The Transformation

The Next Step Up

The Art of Instant Stress Release

How to use your innate powers to create the life you want

Barbara Mahaffey, M.A.

The Next Step Up
The Art of Instant Stress Release
By
Barbara Mahaffey, M.A.

FIRST ENERGY THERAPEUTIC SOLUTIONS EDITION, 2015
San Clemente, CA 92673
Visit our website at www.etsforyou.com

ISBN 978-0-9966622-0-8

Printed in the United State of America

Book Design by:
Jim Biakowski, BookDesign.ca

Medical Disclaimer:
The information contained in this book is not intended to serve as a replacement for professional medical advice. Any use of the information in this book is at the reader's discretion. The author and publisher specifically disclaim any and all liability arising directly or indirectly from the use or application of any information contained in this book. A health care professional should be consulted regarding your specific situation.

Acknowledgements

I am deeply grateful to my dear friend and business partner Debbie Pearson who made it possible for this series of books to be written. Her encouragement, tenacity, sense of humor, editing skills, intelligence and light kept me on tract in writing this book. It has been a wonderful adventure.

My deep gratitude to Andy for his never ending support, motivation, insight, divine wisdom, light, persistence and guidance in the creation of this book.

Thank you Jeff for your insight, editing skills, support, uplifting energy and sense of humor which so greatly helped me in writing this book.

Sheila I have infinite appreciation and gratitude for your editing skills, light, intelligence and genius, wisdom, kindness, thoughtfulness and laughter.

If the above beautiful Souls didn't daily use the tools offered in this book, it would not have been written. We all have the same goal of helping people, beginning with our own selves, to be and to live as True-Self.

CONTENTS

Introduction

Welcome to the first book in the Transformation Series. These books are designed to help you create the best life you really want to live...on the inside, your thoughts, feelings, beliefs and health and on the outside your relationships, your work...basically all your interaction with life. Each book is about The Next Step Up in showing you how to understand and transform what is **not** working for you into what **does** work for you. You will learn easy, yet powerful methods that enable you to make these important life changing transitions easily and wisely.

For more than **thirty years** of being a psychotherapist, I've practiced, taught, lectured and consulted in the fields of traditional and holistic medicine, psychology, business and education. My goal is teaching and **living** the highest use of body, mind and soul in everyday life, everywhere, with everyone no matter what.

After decades of working in multiple health care-fields, I've identified the following areas as most crucial and fundamental to help people help themselves be balanced, clear, happy, healthy and stress-free...both in mind-body-spirit and in the daily living of their personal and professional lives.

These core areas are:
- True-Self or ego...your **choice** of how you think, feel and behave from your True-Self or from your ego
- Energy Awareness...what energy is and how it works for you

- Instant Stress Release…how to stop stressing and shift into calm and clear thinking and acting instead
- Improving Relationships… how to make relationships work, both personally and professionally
- Happiness, Health, Healing and Nutrition…since your health and happiness are greatly determined by what you think, feel and eat, it's how to make wise choices and use energy to expedite all healing

The reason I'm writing the series of *The Next Step Up* books is to give you effective and powerful tools and strategies which show you how to tap into and utilize your innate abilities of Knowing how to be stress free, happy and clear each day of your life plus much, much more.

This book is about The Art of Instant Stress Release. Other books in the Transformation Series include Improving Relationships; Happiness, Health and Healing; Making Easy and Wise Transitions; and Instant Stress Management in a business environment.

The next sentence contains the most important concept you will use in your entire life. **You will be shown how to shift your compulsive negative thinking** (caused by your ego's fearful thoughts and emotions) **into affirmative and confident thoughts from your True-Self.** When you perceive and handle life from your lower-self, the negative ego, your life will seem to be full of conflict, stress and tiredness because that's how your ego makes you think and behave. When you perceive and handle life from your highest-self, your True-Self or Soul or Truth, life will be good, easy and energizing because Soul gives you clarity, confidence and wisdom. You can choose which way you want to live your life… from a low, dense vibratory level, or a high, clear and powerful vibratory level.

If you find yourself functioning from your lower-self, **you will now have the tools to instantly shift out of stressful thoughts and into uplifting thoughts and behavior instead!** You have the power to change and create from the "real you...your True-Self" anytime you desire. You already are the "Real You" on the inside. I just give you the tools and "know how" to access your Soul's power, clarity and wisdom to use any time you choose. Have fun and expect miracles using your innate ability to help resolve problem relationships, work and stressful situations in your life. Remember **it's all in the perception.** When you perceive life from ego, life is hard and stressful. But now you can choose to instantly shift out of being tired and stressed and into powerful and clear perceiving from your True-Self. It feels great...do it often.

There are two fundamental concepts that underlie your change and transformational shifts. The first is *knowing you have a choice in your thinking patterns.* (Even though at times it might not feel like you have a choice, you really do.) You have a choice of thinking, and therefore responding positively from your True-Self, or thinking negatively, then reacting from your ego. In any relationship, situation or anything, you have a choice of perceiving it constructively or destructively. The decision point is only an instant, that's why it seems as if you don't have a choice. If you can't make a decision then you usually go with the dominate habit pattern which is often determined by your higher or lower vibratory level.

The second fundamental concept is Energy Awareness. Do you know *you are designed and structured with natural abilities to sense and work with energy* on multiple levels? Aligning with high energies dramatically increases the positive effect of the transformational work you'll be doing to improve your mind, body and life.

Transformation of the Mind

Thinking from your True-Self or from your ego...
It's your choice
Shifting out of stress and into clarity and calm

After being a therapist for more than thirty years, I've found that everyone's problems are caused from the **same source**—their lower-self's negativity and fear. It's not the actual situation, but their ego's negative perception **about** the situation, that determines if it's stressful or hard. When you **perceive** the same situation from your Truth, it's easy to handle.

These are questions I'm asked time after time: What keeps me living my life from my ego instead of my highest self? Why does my ego seem to have such strong control over me? What keeps me stuck in my ego and stressed out most of the time? How do I live from my highest-self? How can I stay in my True-Self and feel happy and peaceful all the time...or whenever I want?

The answers to these questions lie in how we are designed to function. **As humans we are designed and structured to function optimally from our Souls.** When we do, life works out; when we don't, things seem hard and stressful. So that's *what this whole series is about—how to align with your True-Self and live your life happily and magnificently from your Soul. It's about knowing **how to shift out of ego's negative hold on you and into the calm, confidence and wisdom of your True-Self.** It's also about understanding ego and integrating it back home into your Soul so it can still protect you, but with your Soul's love and wisdom instead of fear.*

The key to making your life work is to know how to align with and easily access the parts of you that innately know how to succeed and excel which come from your True-Self. If you align your mind with your ego, you can expect anxiety, fear and conflict. If you align your mind with your True-Self or Knowing, your life flows smoothly and successfully. Think of the people you know who predominately think and act negatively. Look at the negative people and situations they attract to themselves. Conversely, look at the positively oriented people you know and notice the happy people and positive situations they have attracted.

Energy Awareness

The Art of Working with Energy to Better Yourself and Your Life

Everything is made of energy, including you. You will learn how to sense, feel, be aware of and work with your own energies as well as those around you in the highest, easiest and most appropriate way for all concerned. When your energies are open, expanded and flowing freely, you are happy and healthy. When your energies are constricted, blocked and functioning at a low frequency, you feel bad mentally, emotionally and physically.

You are designed to automatically heal mentally, emotionally, physically and energetically. **The key to healing and functioning from your True-Self is based on your body's energy systems.** Understanding and working with energy through your higher senses is easy and fun because you are structured to function optimally this way.

In this series you will use easy, practical, yet very powerful techniques that are based on how you are naturally structured to excel. You will experience instant feedback on their effectiveness. The hard part is that it's all so easy!

Working with energy is just as important as being able to have your mind shift out of ego thinking and feeling and into True-Self thinking and feeling.

The awareness of and ability to work with Energy is the key to making your whole life work or not work. You're born with the ability to work with your body's natural energy systems. You also have the natural ability to align with high powerful energies that are here helping you be happy, healthy and successful. These high energies are extremely effective in letting you manifest what you want and change what you don't want...both within yourself and in the outside world, especially when you're aligned with your True-Self. These high energies are helping us all to perceive and handle life with Soul's empowerment and wisdom instead of ego's fear and chaos. You'll learn how to align with energies that make life work for you instead of against you.

This book, **The Next Step Up: The Art of Instant Stress Release** is a guide to show you how to shift out of being stressed and into clear thinking and feeling instead. When your mind is controlled by your ego, you experience stress. When your mind is aligned with your Soul, you experience clarity which releases the toxic effects of stress from your body and mind.

In Summary: You will learn how to instantly stop stressful thinking and feeling, which is debilitating and weakens your mind-body, and then shift into a clear, confident mindset instead, which helps heal and strengthen your mind-body. This is all possible because it's how you as a human being are designed and structured to function.

This entire book is filled with powerful methods, tools and exercises to help you make the big shift from your lower self to your higher self. There is a grand finale of high-powered tools in Chapter 5 to make your life work for you in the highest and easiest way. Have fun using these tools.

CHAPTER I

Your Choice of Mindset... True-Self or Ego

There are many definitions of ego, but this is the working one I find most appropriate. Ego is your lowest and densest vibrational self that makes you think, feel and react negatively. When you're perceiving life from ego you automatically react negatively to anything. For example: Your friend calls to chat about her good news. If you are currently in ego you would react by thinking and feeling envious. You hear ego's voice in your head saying, "Why does all the good stuff happen to her and not to me?"

Conversely, your True-Self or your Soul is the highest vibrational part of your being. It wants for you and guides you to what is highest, wisest and best for you... (Throughout this book I will be using interchangeable names for your Highest-Self, such as True-Self, Soul, Knowing, Divine Intelligence or Truth). Your True-Self causes you to perceive and handle life positively no matter what is going on around you. For example: Your neighbor calls to chat about how awful her day has been going. Being in your Truth, you understand how all your friend wants to do is unload her problems on you. You have empathy for her, but don't want to encourage her being a powerless victim. So you turn the conversation in a way that will help her by asking her how she could actually resolve her problems. You encourage her to think and feel positive and strong about herself instead.

The majority of people are not aware that their thoughts and feelings are internally generated from ego or Soul. Most think emotional reacting is just a way of life or that someone or something else is doing this to them…when how you react or perceive actually stems from the inside.

Do you know you have a choice in how you perceive and handle your life…either positively or negatively no matter what the circumstances are? Most people think if something bad is happening they have to feel badly about it. If something good is happening, you should feel good about it, but you really don't so you just pretend to feel good.

Whichever way you choose your mind to think, from your True-Self or the lower-self ego, is the way you will perceive and handle life. **The key to solutions begins in the mind with your choice of how you want your mind to think…positively or negatively.** If you have the belief that you don't have a choice in what your mind thinks, then your subconscious dominate beliefs will make the choice for you since your subconscious beliefs are usually stronger than your conscious ones. Therefore the mind can be either the hero or the culprit. An example of that would be: say as a child you were consistently teased by your older siblings that you were ugly. It hurt and you believed them. Then as you grew up and were pretty, when you looked in a mirror all you saw was an ugly you instead. You wanted to believe you were pretty, but your negatively dominate subconscious beliefs (because they were implanted with strong emotions) overrode your weaker conscious ones. Even though it sometime seems you don't think you have a choice in what your mind thinks, you always do. You always have a choice between negative or positive thoughts. You always have a choice between thinking from ego or your True-Self.

Choosing ego thoughts makes things hard and stressful. Choosing True-Self or Soul thoughts makes things easy and positive. Your choice determines your feelings, behavior, health, relationships, perceptions, stress levels, problems, roadblocks, good events, bad events, etc. You can choose easy or hard … You can choose happy or anxious.

It's always your choice between these two ways of perceiving and dealing with your life. You can make your life hard, stress levels increase, relationships suffer, and health deteriorates if you choose your lower-self or ego. If you choose Truth or Soul instead, your life works, stress disappears, relationships thrive and health quickly improves. If you want **the key** to making your life work… this is it! **Choosing Soul over ego to think, to perceive and to handle your life is the key to happiness, health, good relationships, being stress free, and making your life work for you.**

It's very important to know that you can change how you are thinking and feeling if you do not like what you're thinking and feeling. Most people aren't aware that they can change their thoughts. Have you ever thought about that? Sometimes it's easy to do; sometimes it's hard…depending on your higher or lower vibratory level.

True-Self and Lower-Self (Soul and Ego)

As humans we are designed to function optimally from our True-Self or Soul. Then you feel happy, empowered, whole, and your energy is open, flowing and expanded. Your mind thinks positively which causes your emotions to have a sense of well-being. Conversely when functioning from ego your energy is contracted, constricted and blocked, and you feel fearful, stressed, or anxious and worried. Your mind thinks negative thoughts which cause you to feel negative emotions. What you think determines how you feel. For example if you're thinking about the complement you just got from your boss, you feel happy and proud. If you are thinking about how you got stuck in traffic and missed your flight, you feel angry and frustrated. If you don't like feeling angry and frustrated you can change that easily and instantly any time you choose. You'll learn how to do that very shortly. It really makes you feel powerful to be able do this.

The nature of your True-Self is positive and uplifting

Your Truth is your Higher-Self, or Soul that knows and wants what is highest and best for you all the time. It is always guiding you to be consciously aware of it, and to function from it. With True-Self, or Soul consciousness, we function from awareness, wisdom, love, empowerment, happiness, knowing, and total self-worth. In your True-Self, you do not feel bad or need to worry, nor do you take negative things personally, nor do you seek outside approval and acceptance, because you innately know that as your Soul you are infinitely wise, loving, powerful, understanding and one with all that is.

When your mind runs belief systems that are congruent with your Soul, you perceive, think, and handle life positively and happily which results in being healthy, confident and clear. We are all designed to function optimally when our energy is open, expanded, and flowing. This creates a very high vibratory level which automatically aligns you with even higher energies.

Why is ego so negative?

I am asked this question a lot! This is my understanding and best answer I have for that. Ego's frequency is the lowest and densest of the vibratory levels of Soul. Keep in mind that every part of your being is Soul, even ego. Because we have free will, we are free to experience the whole gambit that exists, from the highest frequency of light and love to the darkest, lowest and densest frequency of negativity...which includes fear, stress, worry, anxiety, greed and power-battles to name a few.

The problem is that it's very easy to get stuck and even lost in ego beliefs, habit patterns and negativity. Sadly ego can trap you into thinking *it* is your real identity, not Soul. You can get so good wearing its costume, you thought you were it. But, thank goodness, you are also designed to override ego's grip on you. There are many ways to do this and you will be learning how to do it instantly and easily. You always have a choice to shift out of ego and into Truth at any time, even if ego tells you it's not possible, it absolutely is instantly possible.

It's important to remember that ego is not your enemy. It's just a part of you that you can easily control with understanding and practice once you know how. There are many ways of handling ego. One of my favorite exercises is to integrate ego back home into the heart of your Soul. It is powerful and feels so good. Remember, the nature of ego is divinely based as Soul, but its functionality is fear based.

The functioning of ego is mostly negative and fear based

The ego's belief structure is predominately fear based. It is structured around power. The ego constantly works to gain power from others but also fears losing its power and control to others. The ego wants to be in control of your mind, all situations, conditions, relationships... of everything, all the time so it can feel secure, strong and powerful. The ego wants you to believe that validation comes from gaining outside acceptance, approval and power from other people, instead of internally from your Soul or True-Self. *When ego can't get control or power from outside sources, it settles for controlling you instead. It tries to keep your mind focused on negative thoughts of stress, worry, fear and anxiety. It thinks the more it can cause the intensity of the pain and stress you feel, the more power and control it has over you.*

Why ego has such a strong hold and control over you

The ego has two very powerful sources that it uses to control you that are very effective. The first is *negative thinking and feeling* which ego has made into strong dominate habit patterns. Unfortunately, in our society about 95% of all habit patterns are ego based. Ego fires off a negative trigger, like worry or anxiety, then off to the races you go. For example: You're driving and a car suddenly pulls out right in front of you, and then proceeds to drive very slowly. Ego immediately makes you think, "How dare he do that to me" (which engages you in an ego power battle with the slow driver.) Then makes you think, "I'll show him. I'm going to pull right in front of him and go slower than he is. Now who has the power? *I DO.*" (Sound familiar? It does to me because embarrassingly, I admit to actually having done this.)

The second source is *ego's ability to control your biochemicals* to make you feel fear, stress, anxiety, worry and being overwhelmed. **Its' biggest asset is its ability to make you believe its lies.** For example: Say your child cuts his hand. Immediately ego makes you think "what if" it gets infected then he could lose his hand. You "know" that he won't lose his hand, but ego is filling your mind-body with fear neuropeptides that make you *believe* he will die. Later when you regain clarity, you think, "Why did I ever believe that?"

The ego's belief system is based on fears

There are 4 behavioral motivation factors of the ego's belief system. Ego knows how to use these basic fears to instill anxiety in you. The worse it can make you feel, the weaker you become and therefore it can maintain control over you. Ego uses the following basic fear beliefs to make you feel badly. Negative or painful thoughts and feelings result from either one or a combination of these 4 fear beliefs:

1. **Fear of being rejected.** The ego believes that if others reject you, you will have to feel hurt. It wants you to believe if you don't get outside validation in the form of acceptance, approval, attention, appreciation, understanding, love, etc., you will feel great emotional pain. (Imagine right now what it feels like if your favorite loved one rejects you. It feels awful doesn't it?)

2. **Fear of not being good enough.** The ego believes that if it can get your mind to run thoughts that you aren't good enough to be approved, accepted, validated, appreciated and understood, you will then feel rejected and hurt. The more hurt it can cause you to feel, the more control and power it has over you.

3. **Fear of loss of power and control.** The ego believes to feel secure, it needs to feel powerful and be in control of situations, conditions, people and you. It is programmed upon feeling powerless or insecure, to evoke whatever behavior it deems necessary to feel powerful again. Aggressive behaviors it often uses to give itself a power fix are anger, justification, righteousness, criticism, blame, and intimidation. Passive ways are by people-pleasing, being the victim, being the rescuer, being aloof, being the fixer. The ego is a master of these behaviors. The ego believes that it needs to be in control of everything. *When it can't, it settles for being in control of how badly it can make you feel to regain its power over you.*

4. **Fear of lack.** The ego believes it will never have enough of whatever it wants, such as power, time, love, money, energy, approval, security, clothes, friends, etc. However much it has of something, it needs more---just one more, to make it feel worthy and more secure.

"What if...?"

There is actually a fifth ego mechanism. It is the *"what if..."* syndrome which can be used to activate any and all fears. It is ego's favorite tool to weaken you. An example would be: "What if I'm not good enough?" What if I can't finish my work on time? What if they don't like me? What if I don't have enough money? Think of how many times you have done this...and how did it feel?

The Levels of ego

The deeper you function in ego, the more negative is your perspective about yourself and your life. **The lower your vibratory level or energy frequency, the more ego wants to fixate and compulse on negative emotions and beliefs.**

On a vibratory level from 1 to 10, one being the lowest and ten being the highest, the following illustrates how the ego functions:

- When functioning at levels 7 through 10, your vibratory level is low, but high enough to return to normal functioning (which is your True-Self or Soul) just by desiring to do so.

- Mid-level functioning at levels 4 through 6 is at an even lower frequency which makes it much harder to get back to Truth or Soul, because ego is so resistant to doing anything positive. It makes your mind confused and muddled (brain-fog), but you still can do it if you are determined.

- At the lowest levels of 1 through 3, it's very difficult to even think at this lowest level, let alone do things to be in Truth again. Down here the ego just wants to wallow in negativity. It sabotages any attempts you make to return to Truth again or even to just feel good.

Ego uses negativity to keep you at a low vibration to control you which makes itself feel powerful.

At these lower vibratory levels *the ego needs to make everything negative.* If positive things occur, it will twist them into being negative. The more negative it can make you think and feel, the more power it thinks it has over you. It looks for justification of why things won't work and why it should make you feel badly about it so it can control you through fear, anger or anxiety. The more you fear, worry and stress, the greater the control it has over you. Recall a time you felt really distressed and down. Did you feel strong or weak? Did it ever occur to you to change your thoughts to positive ones? Why not?

It needs to make you feel badly about how and what you are. It makes you feel guilty that you feel bad and don't want to change it. It tries to make you feel you'll never be good enough. It wants you to feel weak and powerless so it can control of you.

Ego is strong and devious. It knows how to pull you into negative thinking and feeling and will do anything to keep you there. Especially making your think you're weak and can't change your self-defeating thoughts. If you could change your self-defeating thoughts, it knows it would lose power over you and you would have power over it instead. It doesn't want you to know that you are specifically designed to override it at any time. Most people chalk up their negative feelings to "human nature". That it's outside occurrences that make them feel bad, not inside ego habit patterns and perceptions.

Why ego lies to you

Ego is really good at making up lies to trick you into thinking and feeling negatively. It can be little lies like... "See how she's looking at you, that means she doesn't like you!" Or it can be a whooper of a lie like... "That headache means you have a brain tumor." *Ego makes your mind say these things to you in your head.* If you begin to doubt the things it says are not true, it *releases biochemicals to make you believe the lie it just told you is true.* Your Truth is telling you the lie is false, **but the biochemicals make your emotions feel the lie is true.** You get swept away in the emotional fear of it really happening. A little while later when the biochemicals have worn off, you say to yourself, "What was I thinking to believe such a thing?"

Ego makes you think *its* thoughts are *your own* thoughts

Know you *always have a choice* to respond positively with clarity to any negative person or situation. Just because it is a negatively charged situation or person, does not mean you have to feel badly about it. Often you will hear a voice in your head (ego) saying you have to feel worried or anxious because a very bad thing has happened or might happen. Ego wants to trick you into thinking *its* fear thoughts are *your own* thoughts.

Why would you choose negative, helpless, stressful thoughts that do not help you in any way? How is thinking stressfully helping you or the situation? Of course it doesn't help, but ego doesn't want you to think logically or clearly. If you even begin to or want to think clearly, it will release biochemicals to produce "brain fog" or confused thinking so you are unable to think clearly.

Instead of ego's stressful anxious thoughts, wouldn't you rather choose your own empowering thoughts of confidence and wisdom from your True-Self to help you make good decisions? Even if reacting in a stressed way is a dominate habit, you always have the choice to respond with your own empowering thoughts which can override the negative thoughts from your ego. When you find yourself thinking such negative thoughts, stop and ask yourself, *"Do I really want to think and feel this way? How do I want to think and feel instead?*" It seems so simple to do this, but when you're running those negative patterns, it sure doesn't feel simple. You just have to choose to do it.

Here's a very helpful tip: Imagine a time in the past when you felt really emotionally charged about something. Then imagine yourself saying, "*Do I really want to think and feel this way? How do I want to think and feel instead?*" Now in your mind actually notice the difference in how you feel after you've given yourself a choice. You've just taken your power back!

Now imagine a time in the future when you feel yourself jumping in and changing your thoughts to how you want to feel instead. Each time it gets easier to do. Feels good doesn't it!

Ego tries to control you in many ways

Your lower-self ego wants you to feel only what it chooses for you, which is always something painful and stressful. It wants you to believe its lie that you always have to believe what it wants you to believe.

Ego wants you to think *it* is your real identity, not Soul.

Ego wants you to think it's the situation, the relationship, that's hurting you, not *it* hurting you.

Ego uses your mind, your will, your intelligence, emotions and biochemistry for its own good, not for your good. *It projects its own negative thoughts and feelings as yours.*

It doesn't want you to know that you can control it. It uses tools like "brain fog", confusion and distraction to keep you stuck whenever you try to get up and out of it. Ego sabotages any attempt to make you feel better.

The good news is that, because of your self-healing ability, in time the mind and its thoughts will eventually return to Truth. It takes a tremendous amount of your personal energy for the ego to maintain its negative thoughts and feelings. It's like muscles trying to hold up a weight. After a while the muscle begins to weaken and needs to rest to regain its strength. Thank goodness, there are ways of breaking this ego habit pattern and replacing it with positive ones instead. In chapter 3 you will learn techniques of how to do this.

Confusion between Soul and ego

There are times when it seems to be confusing whether one is functioning as True-Self or ego. When your lower-self ego has been gratified and satisfied, a good feeling is often the result. This good feeling can be misinterpreted as coming from the Soul. Although ego gratification can feel good, it's not the deep feeling one gets from being aligned with one's Soul. Notice if the good feelings were derived from outside sources (gaining validation, approval or power from others), or if they originated internally from your Soul. Good feelings from your Soul resonate strongly through your whole being, not just in your mind.

For example: Say you just finished playing a great set of tennis. Every shot you hit was just right, especially your backhand down the line. You felt high from the sheer enjoyment of playing with excellence as your body and mind were in in perfect harmony. You could do no wrong. You could only play with brilliance. It is the sheer joy of expressing excellence in movement and thought. This feeling of expression and happiness came from your Soul.

After the game your opponent complimented you on your play and that made you feel happy too. The first happiness you felt came from your Soul and the second happiness came from outside validation. Which happiness made you feel better?

It is also difficult to determine if you're functioning from your ego or your Truth when you have thoughts that are cautionary in content. You can tell the difference by determining if there is any fear involved. If thoughts came from ego, fear will be present. If they came from your Truth, they just come with a sense of knowing and clear thinking...not with emotionally charged fear.

Here's an example that actually happened to me: I was driving downtown thinking about finding a good parking spot. I turned left then heard a voice in my head calmly say, "Barbara look up." I wasn't really paying attention...had to find my parking spot. Again I heard the calm voice say, "Barbara look up and make a U turn right now." When I looked up I realized I had turned the wrong way on a one way street and cars were heading straight toward me. I calmly made the U turn and was fine. Then my ego took over and screamed at me, "OMG... You dummy, you could have been hit!" Then the calm voice came again and matter of factly said, "You're fine. Turn left at the next block to find your parking spot." Even just writing about that incident after all these years, I can still feel everything that happened then. God bless guardian angels!

Ego is not your enemy

Ego is not your enemy (even though there are many times it feels like it is). Think of it as a wayward child that hasn't received the love it needed and was raised with negativity and the need for power and control. Remember you are designed and structured to override ego any time you choose. Later in the book there is a great technique called Ego Integration into Soul that will help you transition your ego back home into your Soul that feels incredible. I use this method a lot!

Your Soul is your real identity, not ego

Your Soul is the real you. It is your essence. It is light and love and Knowing. Your ego is not the real you. Even though our culture teaches us to identify with the ego to define who we are, it is not true. Your true identity is not ego, it is your Soul. When you consciously experience the happiness of your True-Self, and compare it with the happiness you feel in ego, you can tell the difference. The Soul's happiness is deeply reso- nating, whole and innate. The ego's happiness is superficial, conditional, and dependent upon outside validation and is short in duration. Truth happiness just is. It depends on nothing more than simply being. Ego happiness is dependent on some action or outcome.

The Key to Making You and Your Life Work

This next exercise is one of the most important things you'll ever need to know! It is the key to making everything work. We are designed and structured as human beings to be able to shift out of low thinking, feeling and behaving and into high, clear and confident thinking, feeling and Knowing. It is being able to shift out of ego's negativity and into your Souls light and wisdom where you are calm, centered, strong, clear, happy, peaceful, intelligent and powerful.

There is a subtle difference between "being" Truth and "shift- ing" into Truth. Mostly it's simply a difference of vibratory level. If you're wondering if you are being Truth, you are not in Truth. You know exactly when you are "in" Truth or are "being" Truth by how good you're feeling, how clear you're perceiving and how happy you are.

When you're being Truth, your life just works for you. You don't have to make it work, it just does automatically. It attracts good things for you. For example: When I'm being my True-Self, traffic lights are green. When I'm shopping I find exactly what I want on sale. When I'm working with clients I help them in the most appropriate and powerful way. When I'm riding my horse in the desert, I come across beautiful little quail families. When I'm in a business meeting, things flow and work out beautifully. For me it's a feeling and knowing of being One With All That Is in the highest, easiest, wisest and most loving way.

You can get into the higher frequency of your True-Self by shifting or expanding your energy into a higher vibration that automatically becomes Truth. Then you can perceive and live your life as Truth from your True-Self. This feels so wonderful and easy and right! The following exercise will show you how to do this.

Here is a very simple, yet extremely powerful exercise to center, calm and strengthen you. Simply by expanding your energy up and outward you are designed to feel good. When you contract your energy inward tightly against your body, you feel anxious. By expanding your energy up and outward, you activate your Highest-Self. By pulling your energy inward, you activate your lowest-self. The choice of heightening your energy into Soul or lowering your energy into ego in any life situation is always yours. You might have been taught you don't have a choice, but you always do, no matter what. **This is how we as humans are designed and structured to live, heal and thrive.**

Raising your vibration to shift out of ego and into Truth

(Expanding Up and Out)

You can consciously raise your vibration level to access your True-Self, just by desiring your energy field to expand up over your head by at least 4 feet and by expanding outward from each side by at least 40 feet. Do this from your Knowing not your mind. Your Knowing knows exactly where it is. You mind has to calibrate it and then think…is this right?

When you expand up at least 4 feet over your head, or farther, you use universal energy to function, *not your own personal energy.* (When doing this, you are also aligning with very high energy to make it easier for your angels and high energies to connect with you.)

Expanding out to each side, raises your vibratory level so high, it makes you incapable of accessing stressful feelings such as worry, fear, hurt. You can think negative thoughts, but you can't elicit the corresponding negative feelings. At this heightened frequency you function from your Truth, in which fear does not exist.

EXERCISE

Shifting Out of Ego and Into Truth

Whenever you're feeling stressed, anxious, worried about something and want to be feeling calm, clear, strong, confident and intelligent instead, do the following exercise:

1. **Make a big sigh...** this releases emotionally charged energy.

2. **Look up to the ceiling with your eyes** (don't tilt your head up)... this prevents you from accessing bad feelings. Keep looking up until the emotional "charge" goes away...it doesn't take very long. In most people your brain doesn't access "feel bad" when you look up. You have to look down to access feel bad.

3. **Expand your energy 4 feet up over your head and 40 feet out to both sides**... Use your Knowing not your mind to expand. Your Knowing knows exactly how far out to go. Your mind not so much. Expanding raises your vibratory level so high, you can't feel bad anymore because you have aligned with your Soul or Truth. Feel how calm, clear, centered and balanced you feel now.

How to use this exercise in your everyday life:
For example: Say your co-worker (this works for anyone friend, family, etc.) really annoys you. You find yourself feeling anxious, defensive, or irritated just being around them or interacting with them. But you'd rather feel strong, clear thinking, powerful and intelligent instead. So this is what you do:

Immediately you **make a big sigh** to release the emotionally charged energy you feel. Then **look up to the ceiling** until the emotional charge goes away. Next you **expand your energy up 4 feet over your head and 40 feet out to each side**. Notice how clear and centered you feel now... even with that person still acting annoyingly. You feel free of needing to feel badly when you're with them. You feel calm and clear instead. Now you can interact with them freely with clarity instead of irritation.

Every time you begin to stress about anything stop. sigh... look up...expand your energy up 4 feet and out to each side 40 feet. Right now think of all the situations you can use this tool to shift up and out of stress and into clarity and calm.

Homework for practice: Everyday choose 3 negative situations and do the above exercise. Let one of them be a stressful relationship. Make another one be a situation (like a persistent fear you have of not succeeding, or not being good enough, or not having enough of something like time, friends or money). The third one can be whatever you choose that's bothering or stressing you.

The more you practice this the more you will do it automatically in real life situations. If you do this consistently, it can change your life and give you a freedom from being stuck in negative stressful thinking and behavior. It's always your choice! Act wisely.

In Summary

- The nature of your True-Self is positive and uplifting.

- The nature of low-self ego is negative and fear based.

- Ego needs to control you to feel powerful. It accomplishes this by releasing biochemicals to make you believe its lies and fears. Also it lowers your vibratory level to make you think, feel and behave stressfully. The worse it can make you feel, the stronger and more in control of you it feels.

- Your Soul is your real identity, not ego.

- **The Key to Making You and Your Life Work is:**

1. Know you always have a choice to think and feel positive and strong, rather than thinking and feeling negative and weak, no matter what.

2. Expand your energy up and out to shift out of negative ego and into Souls clarity and wisdom.

CHAPTER 2

Energy Awareness...The Art of Sensing and Working with Energy

(Shhhh…Energy…life's best kept secret)

What is Energy?

Quantum physics has proven everything that exists is made of energy. The earth, the air, water, soil, plants, animals, people, thoughts, lights, electricity, the universe, even an atom are all made of energy waves. Think about this: The largest thing we know is the universe. One of the smallest things we know is an atom. Both have the same structure… planets revolving around a sun for the universe and electrons and protons revolving around a nucleus for an atom.

Each atom has its own unique vibratory level or frequency. Every person has their own distinct vibration or frequency. Every part of you, like your organs, or your digestive system or energy systems have their own unique vibratory levels. When every part of you is vibrating at the right frequency, you feel healthy and happy. When any part of you drops to a lower than normal frequency, you will experience mental, emotional, physical and/or energetic distress.

Each cell in your body is innately designed to know what is beneficial or detrimental to it. All of us, even plants and animals, are structured to communicate through vibrations to sense if incoming energies are good for us or not good for us. Usually plants and animals are a lot better at innately perceiving and reacting to positive or negative energy than humans are. But we still have the ability to discern energies and often use it unconsciously. For example: What would you experience and feel if you walked into a room where people had been arguing and physically fighting? Most would sense at an elemental level that this is not a good place to be and want to leave. We sometimes call the energy waves we naturally sense from other people or situations as being "good vibes or bad vibes".

Using your innate ability to work with energies

Both your awareness of energy and your ability to work with energy, is the key for making your whole life work or not work. Internally you come equipped with the innate ability to work with your body's natural energy systems: energy pathways (meridians), energy centers (chakras) and many vibratory levels or frequencies. Externally you also have the natural ability to align with vibrationally high powerful energies that are here helping you be happy, healthy and successful. You will soon learn how to align with and call to you high energies that help you live from the highest part of you, your True-Self or Soul. They are here to help you perceive and handle your life with wisdom, ease, peace, happiness and light and love. You will learn how to use these high energies to manifest what you want and change what you don't want...both within yourself and in the outside world.

There are infinite energies ranging from the highest vibratory levels to the lowest vibratory levels affecting us all the time. The highest vibrations are congruent and in harmony with your Soul or Highest-Self. The lower realms of vibrations are congruent with negative ego thoughts and feelings. You have the choice of aligning with any vibration you desire and also the ability to shift out of one vibratory level and into another. (Just look at the earth right now. You have large groups of people that are fighting for war and conflict. Conversely you have large groups promoting peace and healing. Guess what vibratory levels they use!)

Strong, yet subtle energies are helping us all to perceive and handle life with your Soul's wisdom instead of ego's fear and chaos. You're free to choose aligning with high energies that help life work for you, or lower energies that make life seem hard and exhausting. These high energies are also helping all of us to *re-integrate ego back home into Soul* so it can protect you with Soul's Knowing, love and wisdom instead. Choose wisely my friends.

Understanding and sensing energy

Energy awareness, as with Truth and ego, has great effect on your happiness, health and life. Everything that exists is made of energy. You are made of energy and have a unique vibratory level. When you're functioning at your proper frequency, you feel happy and healthy. When you're functioning at a lower frequency, you experience negative thoughts and feelings and most likely some physical discord or illness. Your thoughts and emotions are energy too. Everything is energy and emits energy waves.

You are designed and structured with natural abilities to sense all kinds of energies. You are able to tune into people's energies on a mental, emotional and physical level. You can call energies to you. You can send energy from you to anyone or anything. You can align with high loving energy to help strengthen yourself. Or you can align, usually unconsciously, with low negative energy that weakens and depletes you.

Whatever you are emotionally feeling, positive or negative, you broadcast that energy from you. Actually you are *constantly emitting the energy waves of what you feel all the time. This in turn attracts the same kind of energy to you.* So be aware of what you are thinking and feeling. There are infinite ways of sensing and working with energy that are highly beneficial for you. The higher your vibratory level, the easier it is to sense and work with energy.

Your energy waves always sense others' energy waves

You have the innate ability to sense the energy around you just like you use your other senses of vision, hearing, taste, smell and touch. You use this energy sensing ability both consciously and unconsciously to judge if conditions or other people are safe, friendly, or should I be cautious or wary. Whenever you meet a new person, you immediately "scope" them out, or sense if they are friendly or not. Your brain sends out the command that your energy should extend out and feel their energy to see what's going on. *Your words and behavior might convey one thing, but your energy of what you're really feeling contains the Truth.*

Animals do this all the time. Have you ever watched dogs scan a new dog or person or situation with their energy first and then sniff the smell? If the person or dog is friendly, they relax. If the person is anxious or thinking negative thoughts, then the dogs become wary. When you meet a new person, don't you usually reach out and shake hands. Touching them is a way for your brain to calibrate or sense how they "feel". Your energy is simultaneously "scanning" their energy at the same time.

One difference between animals and people, animals are always congruent with their emotions and their behavior. If they like or don't like you, they show it both in their behavior and with their energy. People not so much. They often give "mixed messages". Their behavior and words are often not congruent with their emotions and energy.

You are designed to sense all kinds of energy

Your body-mind naturally knows how to sense all kinds of energy. Everyone processes the input of energy in their own unique way. Some do it visually by seeing it. Some do it kinesthetically by feeling it. Some do it audibly by telling themselves about it. Some do it by sensing it, or just knowing it. Usually it's a combination of all of the above.

Your innate ability to sense energy is subtle, but strong. You can learn to strengthen it with practice. To consciously sense or read or "tune into" energy your mind must be clear and your body at ease. Negative thoughts or anxiety and tenseness hinder your ability to sense others energy accurately.

What your mind thinks, your body feels
You constantly emit the energy of what you feel

Remember your thoughts and emotions are energy too. You are constantly emitting the positive, neutral or negative energy of what you are thinking and feeling. That energy also attracts to you what you're thinking and feeling, both positive and negative. If you're feeling negative emotions you will draw to you the negative energy of others which will increase the intensity of your own negativity. To avoid being affected by others' negative energy it's best to relax your body and clear your mind. This can be done by simply sighing, then remember times when you were very happy. Now feel the difference in your body and mind…way more relaxed and clear.

The next time you go into a room of people, practice consciously tuning into the emotional energy of individuals. Some might be giving off excited energy, or anxious, or bored, or happy energy. Then notice how you react to each kind of energy you experience. It feels good to be around happy people and situations and it feels uncomfortable to be around negative people or situations.

Raise and expand your own energy level to protect you from the negative energy around you

The next step is learning how to protect yourself from other's negative energy by heightening your own vibratory level. When raising your frequency by simply expanding your energy field, others negativity cannot affect you (which means pulling you down into feeling badly too). Most people aren't consciously aware that their energy waves can be pulled up or down when they come in contact with others energy waves. When you are conscious of this action, you have a choice in how to respond. If you don't want to be pulled down with them, then just raise your own energy vibratory level by expanding your energy field. (Remember expand your energy 4 feet up and 40 feet out to each side.) Expanding your energy automatically raises it causing you to be positive and strong instead.

It's interesting to see how negative people react when you do this counter-action. Usually they will try harder to pull you in to control you. If that doesn't work, then they will either turn around and walk away, or join you in a heightened vibratory level which feels good.

You are now learning how to change negative energy into positive energy.

To work with energy, keep your mind clear and positive

Have you ever experienced being trapped in conversation with a negative person? At first you felt fine, then after talking to them you felt negative too. Also have you noticed that when you're feeling negative, you automatically draw others negative energy to you. Not such a good feeling is it? There are many ways to positively and powerfully handle this situation. One very handy and effective way is the ability to change energy from one form into another form...negative into positive.

Before you can change energy forms and even to be able to consciously sense energy, it is essential to have a clear mind and be centered and balanced. It's hard to sense and work with energy if your thoughts are muddled and negative. Once your mind and emotions are clear, it's fun and easy to do. Remember, **you are designed and structured to shift out of negative emotions and into positive emotions automatically** because that is how your body-mind knows how to heal its self.

Having the innate ability to shift out of negative feelings and instantly into positive emotions is one of the most important concepts you will ever learn consciously. You already know it and do it at an unconscious level. The longer you stay in a low vibratory level, the worse your whole body and mind feel which impedes your energy flow. When your energy is blocked, constricted and impeded from flowing freely, it negatively affects your whole being, especially your immune system. Think of it as a toxic sewer backing up... not so pretty.

When you feel "pain"
be aware of what you are thinking

You are designed to "feel pain" physically, emotionally and mentally, to get your attention that you are doing something that compromises your well-being or health. In your normal daily life it's usually chronic and/or acute intense negative thoughts and feelings that are the culprit. We are so used to THINKING AND FEELING NEGATIVELY, that it's become a dominate habit pattern, (thank you ego) that you aren't even aware you're doing it. And so it continues on and on...

Hash Mark Exercise

Do this quick exercise if you think you don't have frequent negative thoughts and feelings. Or if you think you do, but don't know how often you think negatively.

Take out your cell phone and make a hash mark every time you start thinking negatively. Or get a little pad of paper and pencil that you can keep with you in a pocket. Every time you get annoyed, anxious, frustrated, irritated, fearful, doubting, worried, stressed, or start "what-ifing" or experience any kind of negative thinking and therefore negative feeling, make a hash mark on your cell phone or pad. At the end of the day you will be astonished.

One of my favorite clients did it just to prove me wrong. The first day he had so many hash marks he couldn't believe it. So he did it the second day and he had even more hash marks.

Now you finally have an effective way to stop being so miserably stressed. Even if you compulsively worry and fear, you can CHOOSE to make your mind stop worrying and shift into clarity and calmness instead.

If you want to better your life, improve your health, relationships, increase your happiness, confidence and over all well-being, remember to do this EASY and POWERFUL exercise you just learned in the previous chapter: **Sigh...Look up... Expand...** Do this every time you want to shift out of stress and worry and into calm and clarity instead!

The difference between
your mind and your Knowing

When sensing energy, you can use both your mind and your Knowing. Your mind is limited in what it knows. It is governed primarily by your beliefs and the information it has learned. Your beliefs about being open or closed to new information are determined by previously learned beliefs. When you are very young you are open to everything. As you grow older you learn the beliefs of those around you and take them on as your own. That's fine until you come into contact with those who have different beliefs than you. Sometimes that is no big deal, other times it is a very big deal.

You have a choice in having your mind perceive beliefs that are different from yours. Your mind can perceive them either from your True-Self or through your ego. Ego usually uses other people's differing beliefs as an excuse to make you feel bad. Such as making you think the other person is critically judging you. Or that your beliefs are right and others beliefs are wrong which makes you feel righteous. Your ego wants you to engage in a power battle with them to convince them that your beliefs are right and theirs are wrong. Then it goes one step farther in wanting them to change their beliefs to be the same as yours to prove how right you are.

People are often taught in large groups (nations, religions and politics) that their identity and safety lays in their group's beliefs. So when anyone challenges or threatens their beliefs, major strife often ensues. How many wars have been started because of ego's need for power and domination over others?

Your Soul/Truth on the other hand is always open to new viewpoints and never takes differing beliefs personally. Soul doesn't perceive in either right or wrong beliefs. It perceives that they are just "different" beliefs with no emotional charge involved in who might be right or wrong.

Your Knowing is unlimited. Knowing is a high part of your Soul/True-Self that has access to just about everything. It isn't limited to your beliefs, habit patterns, or stored information. For example, if you decided to expand your energy out 16 feet, 21 inches and 41 centimeters, your mind would have to calibrate how far out that would be. Then it would be thinking is it right or did I make a mistake? Your Knowing already knows the correct distance without having to figure it out like the mind and just goes there. Then it gives you the "feeling" or sense that it's at the correct distance.

Your mind has to figure things out. Your Knowing already knows and doesn't have to think about it. If given information, your mind has to think about if it's true or not, then it searches your beliefs to see if the information fits with your belief systems. If it does, it thinks the information is true, if it doesn't, it has big doubts about it. On the other hand, your Knowing just knows if the information is true or not. Whenever you experience anything that is congruent with your Soul, you feel good. All your senses, hearing, seeing, feeling, etc., will be positive. It is a subtle, but strong awareness of goodness or rightness.

EXERCISE

Mind into Knowing Meld

Another good exercise is called the Mind into Knowing Meld. Your goal is letting your mind integrate all the way into Knowing until they are one. You can actually feel this happening inside you. It feels really good and whole.

1. Give a big sigh…Expand 4 feet up over your head…and 40 feet out to each side…

2. Hold your palms up…imagine placing your "mind" in one hand and your "Knowing" into the other hand. Now, move your hands so your palms are facing each other…about 6 to 8 inches apart.

3. Now just sit back and experience your hands as they are slowly attracted to each other. As they come closer and closer feel as your fingertips touch, then both palms will touch. You can sense things happening internally as they touch.

4. When your palms have touched, lay them softly, one on top of the other on your chest. Then breathe them in to the heart of your Soul. Experience how calming, soothing and whole you feel now...

Eventually you'll be able to integrate your mind into your Knowing with ease.

Aligning with High Energies and calling them to you

Energies are infinite. There is energy for anything you can imagine. There are infinite high, loving and powerful energies here to help you be the highest, most loving and wisest that you can be. You can think of them as being broad bands of light and love encircling the earth. Think of anything you need help with and *there is energy to help you in the highest, most loving and appropriate way.*

Energies are easy to align with simply by calling them to you. You begin by turning your palms up. This signifies you are open to calling or aligning with energies. If you don't call any specific energy to you, the default energy that you naturally align with is Universal Flow Energy. That is the high frequency of nature, or Earth. You know how good it feels when you're out in nature... in the forest, or at the beach, or in the mountains...that feeling is this frequency.

Be aware how your palms feel...kind of warm and tingly and full. Now turn them over so your palms are facing down and see how they feel. Do they feel empty? Turn your palms back up. Now they feel full and tingly again. It's the happy feeling of Universal Flow. Imagine when you were a child outside playing feeling happy and excited. Remember just throwing your arms and hands up into the air and laughing…that's the same feeling or frequency of being in tune with nature.

When you turn your palms up and call any energy to you, that energy will fill your palms and the space around you. You can even sense it internally. Sensing energy is fun. It simply takes practice and desire. The more you do it, the easier it becomes. Now you can do at a conscious level what you've already been doing unconsciously forever. It's easier doing it from your Knowing than your mind. The mind wants to analyze what's happening which lowers your vibratory level, while your Knowing just does it naturally. (Here's a tip…when learning something for the first time, let your Knowing show your mind how to do it. To access your Knowing just turn your palms up and say, "Knowing be here now." Notice how you feel lighter, expanded, at peace with a quiet mind that's not chattering…just a beautiful sense of Beingness.)

All energies have their own unique vibration. Even though each energy has its own frequency, they can blend together when needed. You can call just one specific energy, or call to you many energies at the same time. The energies will harmonize to work together for you. It's similar to playing a chord on the piano.

Aligning with your own Soul's energy

Your own Soul has many kinds of energy to work with. Let's begin with calling Divine Beingness (or Soul) Energy to you. This energy is very high, loving, soft, wise and powerful and will be familiar to you because it's your own Soul's Energy. Always begin by sighing…looking up…and expanding your own energy 4 feet up and 40 feet out…(feel free to expand out farther if you want) This heightens your vibratory level and quiets your mind which really helps in aligning with these high energies.

EXERCISE

Calling Divine Beingness Energy, High Functioning Energy and Divine Source Energy

Aligning with these three energies centers, clears and energizes you to do any energy work, or actually anything you want to do or accomplish…even if it's just being happy or quiet…(I use them all the time on just about everything. I tried not using them one day as an experiment and I couldn't do it. I didn't realize how deeply they're wired into me as habit patterns.)

1. Turn your palms up and say, "**Divine Beingness Energy be here now**"…
    You will experience the presence of this beautiful Soul energy in many ways… Let it fill and surround you with light and love and peace…

2. Next call to you **High Functioning Energy.** (High Functioning Energy allows you to function at a high powerful, optimal level.) With Palms turned up say, **"High Functioning Energy be here now"**…You can experience how powerful and clear you are. Whatever you want to do, you can do it from this strong and powerful awareness.

3. Next call to you **Divine Source Energy**. (This energy is extremely powerful and clear.) With palms turned up say, "**Divine Source Energy** be here now"… Sense how really, really good this feels…Notice how quiet your mind is… You feel one with all that is…

Now, from your Knowing, imagine sending these beautiful energies out into your day. Fill your day and yourself with their powerful light and presence...Expect an incredible day...

Another simple, but powerful exercise to **do daily** is:

Aligning with your own Soul

Turn your palms up and say, "**Soul be me now**"...you can feel as your personality and mind recede and beautiful Knowing of love and light fill and surround you. Experience the awesomeness and familiarity of your Soul...Its radiance and oneness with all that is... This is the "Real You"...

Aligning with Resolution Energy

There are many kinds of energy out there to help you with anything and everything. We'll be working with them soon. Right now I want to show you how to work with one of the most helpful of all energies...**Resolution Energy**. Look at all the problems, situations, relationships, conditions, etc. that you are having an issue with on a daily basis. They can be small to gigantic problems...it doesn't matter to the Universe. It can handle anything. Any time you want anything resolved, use this energy!

In my practice as a psychologist, this problem is typically a very common occurrence: "*I feel trapped and stuck in a job I don't like and selling what I don't believe in. I feel miserable. What can I do?*" One of my clients was experiencing this exact situation.

As a therapist there were issues and ego habit patterns we had to clear first such as understanding that his ego was making him feel powerless and "not good enough". After clearing ego patterns and other issues, we addressed finding the most appropriate job for him, aligning with Resolution Energy to do so.

EXERCISE

Aligning with Resolution Energy

1. First hold your palms up, then call **Divine Beingness Energy, High Functioning Energy** and **Divine Source Energy** to you to clear your mind and heighten your energy awareness and vibratory level.

2. With palms up, say out loud, **"Resolution Energy be here now..."**
    Wait quietly as this energy comes to you. Feel its strength and power...Imagine it as a powerful band of energy right in front of you. Then continue saying out loud, **"I place my problem into Resolution Energy to work out in the highest, easiest, most loving and appropriate way for all concerned...especially me!"** Feel how the burden has been lifted from you...

3. **Now imagine how it feels to have the whole problem resolved**. See it, feel it, sense it all working out easily and beautifully. Experience how wonderful, easy and powerfully right it feels. This is the energy that actually creates the outcome you want.

Do this exercise whenever you have a problem or situation that you want resolved. Do it immediately when you begin to feel negative or overwhelmed.

Note: After my client did this technique, he sent out new job applications and within 24 hours he got 4 job offers, each one better than the other. He accepted the forth one which increased his salary, cut his traveling time so he could be home with his family more, and he got to do the kind of work he loved doing and believed in.

I have experienced this kind of successful resolution both for myself and my clients more than I can count. Remember to do these exercises from your True-Self at a high vibratory level and not from a low, fearful, needy vibration that comes from ego. If you feel at all needy, simply sigh…lookup…and expand your energy field until you experience your Truth-Self again.

Aligning with High and Powerful Energies

There are infinite forms of energy. These are some of the most commonly used high energies that are here helping you live as Soul. *Aligning with these beautiful energies helps you to reintegrate ego back into Soul, so you can perceive and handle your life with happiness, clarity, ease of being, divine wisdom and love instead.* These Energies also attract to you what you want. If you want good things, then align with these high, powerful Energies to attract and create wonderful things for yourself and others.

- Divine Beingness (your own Soul) Energy
- High Functioning Energy
- Resolution Energy
- Divine Source Energy
- The Specific Energies for what you want
- Ego Transition Energy
- Living your Soul's Purpose Energy
- Financial Freedom Energy

- Good Fortune Energy
- Happiness Energy
- Ease of Being Energy
- Healing Energies

To align with, or call to you *any* energy simply **sigh... look up... expand all the way up and out, turn your palms up** and say, "(*name of the energy*) **be here now...**"

For example:

"Divine Beingness Energy be here now..."

Wait calmly while this strong, yet light and loving energy fills and surrounds you...Notice that you can no longer think. Your mind stops thinking all thoughts...there's only peace, quiet, clarity... oneness with all that is...You can feel as your Soul re-connects with all parts of your being...even ego.

"Resolution Energy be here now..."

Wait calmly as this energy comes to you. Feel its strength and power...
Put whatever problem, situation, condition, relationship, etc. you have into the Resolution Energy (and say the next powerful words out loud) **"I place my problem into Resolution Energy to work out in the highest, easiest, most loving and appropriate way for all concerned...especially me!"**
Feel how the burden has been lifted from you... **Imagine the end result of your problem being resolved and how wonderful that feels.**

"Living My Soul's Purpose Energy be here now..."

Wait calmly as that energy gently fills your whole being and life with the clarity, love, and light of your Soul...This divine energy helps you to live your life guided by your Soul. This is a good one to begin and end your day with.

"Ego Transition Energy be here now..."

Wait calmly as this energy fills you with its light and love. Its purpose is to clear ego beliefs, habit patterns, triggers, and toxins... and finally to transition and integrate your ego back home into the heart of your Soul so it can function from Knowing and love instead of fear and chaos.

"Divine Source Energy be here now..."

Feel how this extremely high Energy fills and surrounds you. You can do anything with this powerful Energy. Feel it resonating with your whole being as it lifts you higher and higher. You can use its resonance to dissolve resistances. You can resonate with it to clear your food or drinks before you eat. You can use it to restore balance in your body-mind. You can fill your life, problems, relationships, work, anything at all with this high powerful energy to restore clarity and balance.

Helping our planet

If you want to help everyone and everything on Earth, you can expand 4 feet over your head or even much higher (do this from your **Knowing**, not your mind). Now align with the high energies that are present helping all of us to live as Soul. Imagine all egos as they are transitioned back into Truth/Soul with such light, love and power. Now imagine how our planet would be if everyone lived from their Soul with peace, understanding, love and wisdom. Do not underestimate how powerful this easy exercise is for the benefit of humanity and all that is...

Align with the Specific Energies
of what you want

First align with Divine Source Energy to be high and clear in choosing what it is you want…such as clearing negative patterns…attracting good fortune… etc. Then simply **call to you and align with the specific energies of your desired result.** Then say, **"Specific energies of what I want** (specify clearly what that is)**, be here now…"** you can sense them immediately. When there is more than one energy, you can feel the differences in them and how harmoniously they work together.(Like playing a chord on the piano.)

Be aware if you are asking from your ego's fear or from your Soul's wisdom. If there is any fear involved, you are asking from your ego which means your vibratory level is low thus making it harder to actually happen. To heighten it simply sigh…look up… then expand all the way up and out. Or you could call to you Divine Beingness Energy, High Functioning Energy or Divine Source Energies. You could do either one or all to raise your frequency instantly, and then call The Specific Energies to you. You may find that some wants drop away because they are simply ego wants.

EXERCISE

Calling to you the Specific Energies
of what you want

For example: Take the common problem of fearing not having enough money.

1. With palms up, align with the specific energies by saying, "**Specific Energies that are a constant flow**

of financial security and abundance...be here now."

Let the energies fill and surround you...then imagine them flowing out in the universe to do their work for you... Imagine and experience what it's like to have more than enough money. (This is the energy that brings it to you.)

To add even more powerful energy use **Resolution Energy** too:

2. Call to you **Resolution Energy** by saying, **"Resolution Energy be here now"**... Then place the whole money situation, including yourself and all ego beliefs about it, into the Resolution Energy, while saying, *"I place my whole money issue into Resolution Energy to work out in the highest, easiest, and most loving and appropriate way for all concerned, especially me!"*

3. **Imagine the situation beautifully resolved**...feel the ease and resolution...and the clarity of your mind.

   You can do the same thing for clearing negative habit patterns. Say you want to stop stressing. Simply sigh, look up and expand...**Call the Specific Energies to clear your habit patterns of needing to stress.** Sense these energies filling and surrounding you. Often you can even feel them working inside you. Now imagine yourself living a life free of stress. Feel the peace and happiness this creates...

Integrating ego back home
into the heart of your Soul

It's important to be careful not to hate your ego or make it the "enemy." Perhaps you can think of it as a wayward child who doesn't know who it really is. It is a part of you, even if it is misguided and often times cruel. The most effective way I know of helping ego is to integrate it back home into the heart of your Soul. The following powerful exercise shows you how to do this.

EXERCISE

Clearing ego's negativity and
integrating it back into the heart of your Soul:

1. First call Divine Source Energies or High Functioning Energy to you…**"Divine Source and High Functioning Energies be here now…"** Wait calmly while these strong, yet light and loving energies fill and surround you…Notice that your mind can no longer think. You stop thinking all thoughts…there's only peace, quiet, clarity… oneness with all that is…You can feel as your Soul re-connects with all parts of your being…especially ego.

2. Call **Ego Transition Energy** to you…**"Ego Transition Energy be here now…"** Wait calmly as this energy fills you with its light and love. Its purpose is to clear ego beliefs, ego habit patterns, ego triggers, and toxins…and finally to transition and integrate your ego back home into your True-Self so it can function as Soul.

3. **Imagine placing your ego into your palms, then place your palms together in a cupping position... Move your hands slowly towards your heart...As your palms touch your heart, breathe your ego into the heart of your Soul**... to become one with Soul... Feel how clear and peaceful you are now...

Daily Affirmations

- I choose being happy and healthy and wealthy and free... that's me!
- I choose perceiving and handling my life as Soul instead!
- I choose releasing all ego habits and replacing them with Soul instead!
- **Be clear about what you want...Align with the energies for it... Then Expect Miracles...**

In Summary

- Everything that exists is made of energy
- Both your awareness OF energy and your ability to work WITH energy, is the key to making your life work or not work
- You're designed with natural abilities to sense and work with many energies
- Your energy waves are constantly sensing and reacting to others energy waves
- What your mind thinks, your body feels
- You constantly emit the energy of what you're feeling out into the world
- Raise your own energy frequency to protect you from the lower energies around you

- Clear the mind and emotions of negativity, then shift into calm, centered clarity instead
- Your mind is limited, your Knowing is unlimited
- Call your own Soul's Divine Beingness Energy, High Functioning Energy and Divine Source Energy to help you with every thing
- Use Resolution Energy to help solve all problems
- Call Specific Energies to help you
- Integrate ego back home into the heart of your Soul

CHAPTER 3

The Art of Instant Stress Release

How to create your own Instant Stress Release

A problem arises when you feel "stuck" in the habit of perceiving and handling life in a negative and stressful manner. Sometimes you may be stuck stressing temporarily, or sometimes for a long period of time. An example of this is a common belief that when bad things happen or even might happen, you then have to feel badly and be stressed about it. Do you find yourself thinking, "Even though the bad thing hasn't actually happened yet…it might, so I need to start worrying about it now?" How does that stress belief really help you? Of course that negative pattern of thinking doesn't help. It only hinders and weakens you mentally, emotionally, physically and energetically.

This book offers you easy and effective ways to never have to stress like that again. You're designed as a human being to override any pattern of needing to stress in a harmful way. You are also structured with the ability to both change stress habit patterns and release the toxic effect stress has on your body and mind. Your body-mind is innately designed to heal itself if anything harms it. The effects of stress are indeed harmful to your being. The problem begins when you stress faster and more acutely than your self-healing ability can heal you. Then you need help.

After many, many years of watching people suffer the effects of stress (including myself), I have compiled my favorite and most effective techniques, methods, exercises and strategies to help free you from being stuck in stressful thinking and feeling habit patterns. Most of these techniques are mine. Some are from other sources and some are combinations of both. I use whatever methods and combinations that are the most effective for the person or situation. When you use these techniques, you'll experience immediate feedback of their effectiveness. It's fun learning how to let your mind work for you instead of against you. Welcome back good life!

The Goals of Instant Stress Release

1. **It's very important to know how to identify when, where and how you are stressed**. Do you know where and how you feel stress in your body...in your mind?
   Usually stress first begins in the mind with negatively charged thinking. When you think negatively, you feel negatively. When you feel negative emotions, your body reacts by contracting. You experience muscle tension, blocked energy flow, and general dysfunction throughout your body and mind. Most people are so used to feeling stress, they are not aware of how deeply stressed they really are. Again most people don't have a clue how to instantly release their poor stressed body and mind. Until now...!

2. **You need to be able to instantly interrupt the stress loop response by shifting your thoughts from ego caused stress to your Highest-Self's clarity and centeredness**. It's important to understand that feeling stressed is a signal to shift from your lower-self to a clearer, healthier way of functioning. Equally important to understand is how the body-mind

is structured to naturally heal itself when stressed, then utilize your innate abilities to stop stressing and clear its toxic effects from your body and mind. Bye-bye tension headaches, ulcers, digestion problems, and muddled thinking.

3. **Because daily life is filled with challenging situations, conditions and people, you need to know how to perceive and handle stressful situations, both professional and personal, in a clear, centered, confident manner.** Also it comes in handy being able to communicate effectively in any stressful relationship. Imagine right now how you would live if you were stress-free...feel the happiness, freedom and healthy body and mind... Goodbye stress and hello great life!

Health and Happiness vs Stress... Your choice of how you use your mind

As humans we are designed and structured to work perfectly as long as we function within that design. You are structured to work perfectly (1) when all parts of your being are functioning in alignment and congruent with your True-Self; (2) when your vibratory level is high and your energy is open, flowing, and expanded; and (3) when you let go of belief systems that are incongruent with your Truth or Soul. Then you feel happy, healthy and energized.

The core of your being is your innate intelligence...True-Self or Soul. It is the innate intelligence of Soul that knows how to heal you. It is your true identity. It is the highest, wisest part of your being. It is happiness, Knowing, empowerment, and health. It wants for you, and guides you to, what is highest and wisest for you.

You are designed so that when you are *not* in alignment with your Truth, you feel uncomfortable and stressed. The feelings of discomfort, pain and stress, act as a warning devise to (1) get your attention that you are out of congruence with Truth and (2) to motivate you to shift back into alignment which immediately alleviates the discomfort. Usually it's the running of ego fear beliefs that most often keeps you out of congruence. The longer you stay out of alignment, the worse you feel and the greater your well-being is compromised.

The state of your happiness, health, and the ability to calmly handle stress is determined by your belief systems. Aligning with Knowing keeps you happy and healthy. Unconsciously running negative fear based beliefs creates stress and dysfunction.

Your beliefs determine your thoughts. Your thoughts determine your emotions, reactions and behavior.

For example, say you have the negative ego belief, at the conscious and/or subconscious level, that you need outside validation and approval in order to feel happy or good about yourself. If someone rejects you or you think they might reject you or your work, your thoughts will reflect that belief by being negative. Running negative thoughts and feeling the corresponding emotional pain causes stress and dysfunction throughout your entire being. The emotional discomfort greatly increases if you try to repress or stuff your negatively charged feelings.

How ego causes you to stress

What takes you out of congruence with Truth most often is your ego and its fear based beliefs. The majority of your beliefs are negatively programmed through your ego. Unfortunately, most of our society is ego oriented. That's why we have so many fears and power struggles and stress. Whenever you run negative thoughts and emotions you become stressed.

The ego's functioning is based on these basic fears:

1. **Fear of being hurt or rejected.**

2. **Fear of not being good enough.**

3. **Fear of loss *of power and control*.**

4. **Fear of lack.**

5. **Fear of "what if..."** What if I'm not good enough? What if I can't do it right? What if they don't like me? What if... and on and on...

All of your negative feelings are based on one, or a combination of these elemental fears. Whenever these fear beliefs are triggered, the ego makes you feel powerless and therefore throws you into passive or aggressive behavior to regain the illusion of being powerful. When the ego can't control or have what it wants, it settles for controlling you by making you feel bad. It does this because it knows how to control your mind to think negative thoughts which weaken you and therefore make it feel powerful. When it gets what it wants, it feels good...but only temporarily.

Your beliefs and perceptions define your stress

What you perceive as stressful is determined by your beliefs. What is stressful to one person may not be stressful to another depending on their beliefs about stress. For example: Addressing a large audience may be extremely stressful to one person and be actually fun for another. **It's *not* the event that affects you, but *how you perceive* the event and the beliefs you run about it that determines its effect on you.**

When thinking fear based beliefs you experience stress, anxiety or pain. The body is structured to use pain as an attention getting devise to warn you that you are out of congruence with your Truth. Because it's sometimes too emotionally uncomfortable to feel pain or anxiety, you tend to repress its negatively charged energy which causes even more pain. *You are designed to naturally release charged energy by sighing, looking up, laughing, breathing, jiggling and crying.* I'm sure you've noticed that when anxious, men tend to jiggle (especially the change in their pockets) and women tend to nervously giggle. *To release extremely charged energy you curse, yell and engage in big motor activities* like running or throwing things.

If you didn't naturally release this charged, stressful energy, you would feel like a pressure cooker ready to explode.

How ego affects your stress

Stress is caused by the *ego's inability* to control all the situations, people, conditions, and relationships that it wants to control. Whenever the ego can't have what it wants, it feels powerless. *When you feel powerless or overwhelmed mentally, emotionally, or physically, you feel stressed.* Whenever you are actually threatened, or *just fear* being threatened, the brain is triggered into the emergency response condition of fight, flight or freeze. *This crisis response is the same whether you experience a real physical threat, a fear of being rejected, a fear of not being in control, or daily irritations and frustrations.*

The Stress Response

The body usually reacts to your lower-self's fear of emotional threats the same as if they were real physical threats of danger. It has a negatively charged emotional reaction whenever it can't control or do what it wants. This negative emotional response (stress response) is experienced throughout your body----in your organs, systems, biochemistry, even your perceptions. It weakens everything, from not being able to think clearly, to greatly weakening your immune system. Because your daily life behavior is dominantly governed by your ego's fear beliefs, the stress response is stuck in the "on" position most of the time which plays havoc with your health, your emotions and your ability to think and perceive clearly.

How the stress response works

Chronic stress causes negative consequences both emotionally, mentally and physically, eventually debilitating the immune system as well as hampering your ability to cope successfully with life. Stress response hormones and chemicals pour into your bloodstream leaving you feeling more fearful, anxious, angry or aggressive than the situation may warrant.

When the stress response system, which is your fight or flight mechanism, kicks in most of your blood leaves your forebrain, which reduces your capacity to think clearly. (Later in the book you will learn specific techniques to counteract this situation.)

When people are in situations that are *perceived* to be threatening for sustained periods of time, the sympathetic nervous system stays activated, overtaxing your body and emotional well-being. This continued activation reduces your ability to relax even when circumstances normalize, thus causing the habit pattern of being continually fearful or "on guard." You fall into the stressing habit of the "what if…." syndrome. "What if" something terrible is happening or going to happen.

There is a specific technique you can use to clear a fear case of the "what ifs…" This technique (Exit Loop 4) can be found in the next section "Exit Loops Out" of ego's negative thinking.

How You Can Change the Stress Response Loop

Fortunately you are naturally designed and structured to automatically heal anything that is out of balance or in dysfunction. In addition to being warned that you are thinking in patterns that are not conducive to your well-being, you are also designed to shift your thinking from the negatively charged thoughts (of your lower-self) to clear thoughts and the emotional balance of your higher-self.

Over the years I have developed the Exit Loop Out of stress techniques as I observed how effective they were. Each technique utilizes your innate ability to shift out of stress and into balance instead. **These easy-to-use strategies are highly efficient Instant Stress Releasers for your everyday life both personally and professionally.**

I promise you if you use these easy techniques every day, it can change your life. They are specifically designed to let you control your mind to do what you want it to do, not what your lower-self wants it to do! It gives you the freedom from needing to stress. You can respond to stressful situations with clarity, ease, calmness and confidence instead. They really work. The more you use them, the stronger they become. You are changing the dominate stress habit pattern and replacing it with the new pattern of peace and clarity instead.

How to use Instant Stress Release techniques

Exit Loops out of negative thinking stops stress in its tracks

How often have you found yourself stuck running negative thoughts over and over again, like a hamster running in circles on its wheel? If you're thinking and feeling negatively, then you are experiencing stress! Whenever you're caught in negative thinking or compulsing, the following techniques **are exit loops out of the hamster wheel and into freedom and peace. Every time you use** any of the exit loop exercises, always begin by sighing, looking up and expanding your energy 4 feet up over your head and 40 feet out to each side. This puts you in a centered place to do these exercises.

To instantly STOP thinking and feeling negatively, and shift into thinking clearly, do one or any combination of these Exit Loops out of stress exercises.

Exit Loop 1 is the best one for just about everything. You can use it for all stressful situations. Usually after the fourth step you feel clear, but if you still feel a little charged, do all seven steps for the best results.

Exit Loop 1

The Best "Go To" Combination for Everything

1. **Sigh... and look up at the ceiling** (only with your eyes, not your head)! Continue looking up until the emotional charge clears.

2. **Expand your energy 4 feet up over your head** and **40 feet out to each side**...(or farther if you want) *If you still feel emotionally charged, continue with the following:*

3. Say. **"DO I WANT TO FEEL THIS WAY...NO!"**...

4. Say, **"I CHOOSE happiness, clarity, peace, divine wisdom and strength INSTEAD!"** Notice how powerful and clear you feel ...

5. With palms up, Say, **"High Functioning Energy** and **Divine Source Energy be here now"**...Feel the peace, clarity and strength of these powerful energies..."

6. **Clear** the **negative feelings** and **transition ego back into the heart of your Soul:**

   Extend your arms out in front of you. Imagine placing your ego into your palms then placing one on top of the other... Move your hands slowly toward your heart...As your palms touch your heart, breathe your ego into the heart of your Soul... to become one with Soul. Feel how clear and peaceful you are now...

7. Say, **"Resolution Energy be here now"**. Put your problem into the energy and say, **"Problem I put you into Resolution Energy to work out in the highest, easiest and most loving and appropriate way for all concerned...especially me!"** Feel how all the stress is gone and the burden has lifted... **Then imagine how it feels when the problem is all resolved**...experience how clear and happy you feel... *(This last part of imagining how good you feel when it's all resolved is very important because that's the energy that creates what you want!)*

Exit Loop 2

Twirling

If you are **really angry or stressed and** you need to instantly *reboot your brain* **to clear your feelings when they become too intense.** Do this by:

Twirl (spin in a circle) 3 times one way, then 3 times the other way. (It's OK if you get a little dizzy...it still works to clear your brain.)

Exit Loop 3

Frontal Touch (Overriding Ego's Control)

To override or transcend your ego's negative control of your mind, do the following:

Think about the issue, or feeling or situation that is troubling you...

1. **Place your thumbs on your temples. Then lay your fingertips horizontally across the center of your forehead**...This causes blood to flow back into your frontal cortex so you can think clearly.

2. Wait for your charged emotion to dissipate...it doesn't take long.

3. Command your *ego* to say the following, "**I choose my Truth** (or Soul)...**always!!**" Now feel how clear, centered and strong you are.

Exit Loop 4

Clearing the "what ifs" with "Prove to me your lie is true!"

1. Ego will tell you any lie to get you to feel weak and powerless so it can control you. It's favorite fear and worry tactic is to say to you, **"what if"** something's wrong...**what if** you aren't good enough...**what if** they don't like you...**what if** it won't work...**what if** something terrible is going to happen...

2. As soon as ego starts with the **"what ifs..."** You say to it, **"Prove to me your lie is true!"** It never can, because it always lies. You can feel it receding immediately. If you **consistently interrupt** it with **"Prove it to me"**, it won't want to use the "what if..." tactic anymore because when if it does, it loses its power to you.

Exit Loop 5

Soul Fountain (very powerful)
Clearing Negative Thoughts, Feelings & Energies

This exercise is especially good if you're in a toxic situation, or around a toxic person, or in an argument with someone.

Give a big sigh, look up and expand 4 feet up and 40 feet out.

Imagine your Soul's light and love flowing up and out of you like a fountain. As the light flows up and out of every pore, it takes with it all negative energies and toxins that you have suppressed. Releasing and clearing everything...leaving you feeling clear and refreshed...with a deep feeling of well-being. Do this as many times as needed throughout the day. Remember to do this before you fall asleep at night. You will have a wonderful night's sleep.

Exit Loop 6

Confronting and Clearing Ego with "NOW WHAT" (very powerful)

Whenever ego is making you fear say, **"OK, ego suppose you're right...NOW WHAT?"** As you say "now what", lift your hands up and use them emphatically. Ego will immediately back off and recede because it got caught lying. You took its power away and gave it back to yourself.

Check to see if there's any remaining fear. If there is, check to see what the percentages are...Example: 80% gone, 20% still there. Continue repeating the exercise until the fear or charged emotion is completely gone.

Exit Loop 7

Calling Your Soul's Energies to You

Whenever you **need a lift, energy boost or want to feel high and clear** do the following:

Lift your palms up and say," **Divine Beingness Energy be here now..."** Feel how light and powerful you have become... Now say, **"Divine Source Energy be here now..."** Feel how centered and strong you are. **"High Functioning Energy be here now..."** Experience how powerful, peaceful, integrated and confident all these high energies make you feel...

Exit Loop 8

Soul Merge

You are made up of all different kinds of parts...your mental and emotional and physical parts. You want to have all of them working congruently and this exercise does that.

To have all aspects of your being be in harmony with your Soul, do the following exercise:

1. Hold your palms cupped together out in front of you.

2. **Imagine placing your ego into your palms**... Move your hands slowly toward your heart...As your palms touch your heart, breathe your ego into the heart of your Soul... to become one with your Soul.

3. With your palms cupped and outstretched, **imagine placing your personality into your palms**... Move your hands slowly toward your heart...As your palms touch your heart, breathe your personality into the heart of your Soul... to become one with your Soul.

4. **Now imagine placing your thoughts and your feelings into your hands**... As your palms touch your heart, breathe your mental and emotional parts into the heart of your Soul... to become one with your Soul.

5. **Imagine placing your physical self into your palms**...as your palms touch your heart, breathe your physical self into the heart of your Soul... to become one with your Soul.

6. **Finally imagine placing your subconscious into your palms**... As your palms touch your heart, breathe your subconscious into the heart of your Soul... to become one with your Soul.
Feel all of your being in harmony with your Soul...feeling whole and complete...Feel how clear and peaceful you are now...

Exit Loop 9

Transitioning Ego Back Home into Soul (very powerful)

First hold your palms up, then call High Functioning Energy by saying, **"High Functioning Energy be here now..."** feel how wonderful it feels...

Then say, **"Ego Transition Energy be here now"**...feel how strong this energy is...

Now proceed with the following steps:

1. Imagine your ego in one hand.

2. Imagine you Soul in the other hand.

3. Face your palms each toward the other. Now just watch your hands as they slowly begin to draw toward each other. You can feel as your Soul hand begins to fill the ego hand with Light and love. Slowly your fingertips, then your palms will touch. As this happens you can feel subtle changes happening internally.

4. Let your hands naturally fold over each other as they lay on your chest. Breathe in the peace and wholeness you feel.

Exit Loop 10

Melding the Mind into Knowing

Showing your mind what it feels like to be one with Knowing...

1. Put your mind in one hand and your Knowing in the other hand...feel the difference between the two... your Knowing hand feels stronger and lighter...your mind hand feels a lot heavier...

2. Face your palms toward each other and let your mind hand be filled with Knowing's light and wisdom... as your palms touch, your mind is now guided by your Knowing...feel the congruence and ease of being and experience how quiet your mind is now.

Exit Loop 11

Make Hashtags Each Time Ego Makes You Think Negatively

Make yourself aware of how many times you actually think negatively during the day...It will astound you...Plus when you stop to make the hashtag, (on your cell phone or paper) you interrupt the negative thinking habit pattern. Now is a good time to **sigh and look up and expand** to clear your negative thinking.

Exit Loop 12

The Energy Bubble or Energy Field

Use "The Energy Bubble" or Energy Field to stay clear and unaffected when surrounded by the lower vibrational energy of people or conditions.

Here is the process for doing that:

Whenever you are in a situation, both personally or professionally, that is really negative, you can protect yourself from being negatively affected by using "The Energy Bubble" or Energy Field.

This is very effective when you're stuck in a conversation with a person strongly rooted in ego who won't stop talking.

1. First construct an Energy Bubble for yourself, then more bubbles for whoever needs them. To do this, first check your vibratory level. If you're experiencing any uncomfortableness or anxiety, you need to raise your frequency simply by sighing...looking up...and expanding up and out...or aligning with your Soul's high energy.

2. Imagine yourself being surrounded by a beautiful Bubble of Light. Fill the Bubble with Divine Source Energy and High Functioning Energy or any high energy of your choice. Because your energy is now calm, clear, confident and aware, you don't take anyone's remarks personally. You radiate positive energy. You can make your Bubble as thick or thin as you choose depending on the situation.

3. The outside of your Bubble neutralizes all negativity that comes your way.

4. Tune into the energies of those around you. For those that are radiating negativity...demeaning, arrogant, judgmental and annoying, etc., you can surround them with their own Bubble of Light and Love. The inside of their bubble reflects back to them awareness of their own negativity and how it affects others. It helps to open their ability to be insightful and not want to be negative anymore.

When working with people who have contentious relationships, I always use Bubbles for myself and for them because the Bubbles really work.

Exit Loop 13

Opening Your Chakras (very powerful)

What are chakras?

Chakras are major energy vortex centers. They're spinning wheels of *energy* located on the midline of your body. There are seven major chakras in the body and many more minor ones as well as chakras above the body. When your chakras are not open and flowing with energy, you cannot function well mentally, emotionally, physically or energetically. You feel sluggish and it's hard to think clearly. It especially compromises your immune system.

The Crown Chakra

The 3rd Eye Chakra

The Throat Chakra

The Heart Chakra

The Solar Plexus Chakra

The Sacral Chakra

The Root Chakra

Your **Crown Chakra** helps you to be fully connected spiritually, especially with energies of light and love. It's located on the top center of your head.

Your **Third Eye Chakra** deals in inspiration, imagination, wisdom and comprehension in totalities. It's located in the center of your forehead.

Your **Throat Chakra** helps you to communicate and express yourself. It is located in the throat area.

Your **Heart Chakra** helps you experience the highest forms of love. It is located in the center of your chest just above your heart.

Your **Solar Plexus Chakra** deals with emotions, self-confidence and self-worth issues. It is located in the stomach area of your abdomen.

Your **Sacral Chakra** deals with pleasure, sexuality, connection to others and new experiences. It is located about 2 to 3 inches below the naval.

Your **Root Chakra** helps you feel grounded and stable. It is located at the base of your spine or tailbone.

To open your chakras, place the fingertips of both hands on the center of your chest, then extend your arms all the way out with palms turned up. Open and close them rapidly until your chakras begin to open and clear and you feel open and lighter. Next, do the same with your Throat Chakra, then your Third Eye Chakra, then your Crown Chakra (located on the top of your head), then your Solar Plexus Chakra (about 3 inches above your naval), then your Sacral Chakra and finally your Root Chakra (about 3 inches below your naval).

Exit Loop 14

Releasing Endorphins, Serotonin and L-Dopamine to counteract ego's stress

Whenever ego releases bad feeling biochemicals, you can instantly counteract that by saying, **"Knowing, release endorphins, serotonin, L-Dopamine and norepinephrine NOW!** You can feel instant relief right away. If you need more, just command it to release more until you feel comfortable again.

Another very effective method is the release of Forced Attention which causes anxiety and stress

Forced attention or denied attention causes resistance and stress. Your attention is attracted to where it wants to go and repelled by where it doesn't want to go.

Any time you try to keep your attention on something that it no longer wants to focus on (by using your will to keep it there), you will experience resistance. When the attention's resistance is stronger than the will's force to keep it focused, you will experience exhaustion, being overwhelmed, anxiety and confusion—until the attention can finally be released to go where it wants to go.

Resistance is trying to put or force your attention to where it doesn't want to go.

The opposite is also true about resistance. When your attention wants to stay (especially fixate or compulse) on something and you force it away, you will again experience resistance.

When attention wants to fixate on something and you force it to cease by repressing its energy flow and stuffing it, you will experience constriction and discomfort until it can freely express itself again. The best way to change your attention from fixating, is to distract it to something else. For example: When compulsively thinking negative thoughts, distract yourself by simply asking yourself, "Do I really want to feel this badly and be this stressed?"

Either forcing attention to go where it doesn't want to go, or not letting attention focus where it wants to, will cause a person to feel stressed.

Exit Loop 15

A quick and useful exercise to release stressful attention

When working on a task, like your computer and the resistance of attention begins to build to an uncomfortable level, stop and look out into the distance. Let your attention go wherever it wants to go. This can be done repeatedly over a period of time in a two step process: focus attention until resistant, then relax, sigh and let your attention wander; focus then relax, sigh and let your attention go. Continue with this until your task has been comfortably completed. (You can also do some charged energy releasing techniques and/or get up and move around.)

In Summary

The major causes of stress

1. **Negative thoughts and emotions are triggers for the stress response**
   For example: Being stuck in negatively compulsive thinking… being stuck in "what if's", and being afraid of health issues. Not being in control and feeling powerless causes major stress issues.

2. **External situations and events that you cannot control such as people and relationships also trigger stress responses.**
   For example: Feeling powerless and or feeling lack of control in situations or relationships. People just won't do what you want them to do. Things aren't working out how you want them to. These cause much frustration and stress.

3. **Forcing of your attention to go or stay where it does not want to go or stay causes stress.**
   For example: When you are working at your computer and your eyes and mind want to look away from the computer, but you force them to continue looking at the computer and stay focused on what you are working on. (Just as mine are doing right now as I am writing this.) As soon as you let them go where they want to go, you experience great relief.

CHAPTER 4

Instant Stress Release using Energy Psychology and Energy Medicine

I nstant Stress Release technology is based on how your body and mind are designed to heal when your thoughts, emotions, brain and biochemicals are affected by your energy systems and electromagnetic fields. It uses the best of both Energy Psychology and Energy Medicine which are cutting edge forerunners in their respective fields of psychology and medicine. They often overlap each other in their methodology and format, but have proven to be highly effective in most situations to help you live a life free of stress.

What is Energy Medicine?

Energy Medicine is using energy for health, healing and happiness in your everyday life. When the energy systems of the body-mind, including energy pathways (meridians), energy centers (chakras) and vibratory levels are all open, flowing and expanded, you experience good health and happiness.

Donna Eden, the foremost expert in Energy Medicine, explains in her book *Energy Medicine*, "Using the principals of Energy

Medicine you can optimize your body's natural capacities to heal itself and to stay healthy. You can manage your energies to more effectively meet stress, reduce anxiety and free yourself of many ailments."

David Feinstein, Ph.D. states in the book *Energy Medicine*, "Conventional medicine focuses on the biochemistry of cells, tissue and organs. Energy Medicine, at its foundation, focuses on the energy fields of the body that organize and control the growth and repair of cells, tissue and organs. Changing impaired energy patterns may be the most efficient, least invasive way to improve the health of organs, cells and psyche."

What is Energy Psychology?

As stated by Dr. Fred P. Gallo, in his book *Energy Psychology*, "Energy Psychology is the relationship of energy systems to emotion, cognition, behavior and health. These systems include electrical activity of the nervous system and heart, meridians, chakras, energy fields, etc.

Although psychological functioning involves thought, emotions, chemistry, neurology, genetics and environmental aspects, at an essential level bioenergy is involved. Just as an audiotape or a computer hard drive contains information in electromagnetic fields; similarly our brain and body operate electromagnetically. Energy Psychology is applicable to a wide range of areas including psychotherapy, counseling, education, physical health, pain management, sports and peak performance."

Thought Field Therapy

Thought Field Therapy is a branch of Energy Psychology that deals with the interrelationship between emotions, thoughts, behavior and the body's energy systems. By tapping into specific points of the body's energy systems, emotional, mental and physical stress can be cleared. Limiting and negative beliefs, thoughts and habit patterns can be cleared or reprogrammed into ones that are congruent with your innate intelligence or Truth.

The body-mind is structured and designed to automatically heal itself, physically, mentally, emotionally and energetically whenever an imbalance occurs. For example, when you physically cut yourself, your body-mind knows innately how to go about healing the wound.

Emotionally when you think negative thoughts, you feel corresponding negative emotions which cause your body and its systems to be compromised. These discomforts will often times cause you to want to hold or rub your forehead or temples. This is where certain neurovascular points are located which when touched, are designed to clear the emotional charge and restore you to emotional clarity. When you are emotionally over-charged and anxious, you are designed to automatically sigh, laugh, yawn, jiggle and cry to release charged energy.

There are many specific points on the body that are designed to naturally clear charged emotions and energy, especially energy that has been stuck or repressed. These points are located on meridians that are energy pathways which flow through the body. When these points are massaged or tapped, they clear the emotional charge you are experiencing so you can return to normal functioning.

If you are worried about a situation, stimulating these points (by tapping, massaging, or holding) shifts your perceptions from the negative viewpoint of worry, which is limiting and debilitating, to perceptions that are clear, neutral or positive, so you can handle the situation in a positive manner. The body-mind is designed and structured to restore you to normalcy and balance…to clarity and health.

The next two exercises are examples of Energy Medicine and Energy Psychology techniques:

Exercise

Tapping and Eye Roll Technique

This Tapping technique releases the charged energy you experience in a negative situation. It also stimulates the brain to begin replacing the undesired habit pattern of negative thinking and feeling into a positive one instead.

Think about the problem or person you want to change your negative reaction to and breathe a *big sigh* to begin releasing any emotionally charged energy.

1. Begin continuously tapping on the back of your hand on the spot between the knuckles of your little finger and ring finger while tapping and thinking about the problem or person. Then say exactly what you are feeling about the problem or person. For example, you might say, "You annoy me...you annoy me...you annoy me...Keep **saying what you feel** as you are tapping your hand. *You are literally tapping out the bad feeling. After a short while of doing this, you will lose the negative charge altogether.*

2. While tapping, hold your head still and look down at the floor. Then slowly roll your eyes to look at the wall to your left, then up to the ceiling, then to the wall on your right, then back down to the **floor. Next, look again to the wall on your left, ending by looking up** at the ceiling. You have just made one and a half revolutions with your eyes.

3. Breathe a big sigh and check to see if there is any

remaining charged feeling. If not, you can now perceive and handle the situation with clarity from your Truth.

4. If there is any charged emotion remaining, repeat the process of tapping, eye rolling and repeating what you feel until the emotional charge has dissipated.

This particular technique reminds me of a client who used this method very effectively when he was annoyed with a certain employee. He didn't want to feel annoyed; he wanted to feel happy and calm when in his employee's presence. Whenever he saw this person coming toward him, he said, "Oh, oh, here comes Leroy" and started to tap vigorously on his hand while saying to himself, "you really annoy me...you really annoy me... After several times of doing this, every time he saw Leroy, he felt great!

The above technique deals with the interrelationship between emotions, thoughts, behavior and the body's energy systems. **By tapping on specific points of the body's energy systems, emotional, mental and physical stress can be cleared. Limiting and negative beliefs, thoughts and habit patterns can be reprogrammed into ones that are congruent with your body-mind's integrity and well-being.**

It is very important to be able to stop the stress responses continual looping affect. The above technique and the following technique teach you to instantly get back to centeredness (Truth) and to stay there and sustain it. Learning to stop the feeling of stress right in the moment helps the immune system from being compromised.

Frontal Cortex Automatic Calming and Centering

The brain needs an adequate amount of blood flow to function properly. As Dr. Candace Pert, a foremost neuroscience researcher, states in her book *Molecules of Emotion*, "Blood flow is closely regulated by emotional peptides, which signal receptors on blood vessel walls to constrict or dilate and so influence the amount and velocity of blood flow…If your emotions are blocked due to denial, repression, or trauma, then blood flow can become chronically constricted, depriving the frontal cortex, as well as other organs, of vital nourishment. This can leave you foggy and less alert, limiting your awareness and thus your ability to make decisions that change physiology or behavior. As a result you become stuck---unable to respond appropriately to the world around you, repeating old patterns of (negative ego) behavior…"

The following Energy Medicine technique is how the body-mind naturally heals itself by shifting your thoughts and emotions to those of health and well-being. Also by releasing repressed toxic emotionally charged energy so the body-mind can return to normal functioning.

Exercise

Frontal Cortex Centering and Clearing

Whenever you have a negative thought and feeling, or begin to feel stressed about a problem do the following exercise to be centered and clear:

- **Stop and SIGH…then look up…** Sighing releases charged emotional energy. Most people are not wired to access charged emotions when they look up.

- **Put your attention in your frontal cortex (forehead)…** This part of the brain is responsible for higher functions such as making decisions, intentions to change, judgments, planning future acts, etc.

- **Now put your attention on your heart beating calmly and rhythmically in your chest...** This causes you to relax and be calm.

- **Put your attention back in your frontal cortex...** This strengthens conscious control of the autonomic system for the next command regarding blood flow.

- **Put your attention on your blood flowing into your hands and fingers...feel them becoming warm and tingly...** This normalizes blood pressure and is calming.

- **Put your attention back in your frontal cortex... feel blood flowing to your forehead...feel it becoming warm and tingly...** Flowing blood into the frontal cortex nourishes it so it can perform conscious interventions at the highest level.

- **Put your attention back on your heart beating calmly in your chest...now feel your heart center opening...wide open...and keep on expanding out to each side...at least by 40 feet or farther...** Opening your heart center calms you...Expanding your energy out to each side raises your vibration which gives you a deep feeling of well-being.

- **Put your attention on the top of your head... feel it opening all the way open...now expand up 4 feet...** Opening the top of your head calms you...Expanding up 4 feet shifts you to a higher consciousness and centers you.

- **Breathe a big sigh...and feel how good you feel... now think of the problem...and notice how you feel...** Notice how your perception of the problem has changed...The emotional charge has dissipated allowing you to handle the problem more clearly and easily.

The above techniques deal with the interrelationship between emotions, thoughts, behavior and the body's energy systems. By tapping on specific points of the body's energy systems, emotional, mental and physical stress can be cleared. Limiting and negative beliefs, thoughts and habit patterns can be reprogrammed into ones that are congruent with your body-mind's integrity and well-being.

It is very important to be able to stop the stress responses continual looping affect. These two techniques teach you to instantly get back to centeredness (Truth) and to stay there and sustain it. Learning to stop stress right in the moment protects the immune system from being compromised and the hormonal imbalance and the brain from being foggy and confused.

Science has proven that the heart's rhythm affects the rest of the bodily rhythms, especially the brain. There is a strong link between emotions and patterns of information in the heart rhythm. The information sent from the heart to the brain, as well as to all parts of the body, influences how the brain and the whole body function. Dr. Candace Pert has done extraordinary research on how emotions and their biochemical substrates, peptides, are found in each cell of our body.

How the body, mind and emotions act as one

As Dr. Pert explains in her book *Molecules of Emotion*, "Your emotions are produced by the secretions of specific neuropeptides which are experienced through the whole body. When peptide ligands bind to their receptors which are located on the outside of each cell, there is a biochemical reaction resulting in an emotion. Each emotional state communicates and coordinates an interaction of the body and brain…from facial expressions and behavior to bodily functions. Neuropeptides and their receptors act as biochemical information carriers linking all the organs, systems and processes of the body-mind and brain to work harmoniously.

Your mind is not just in your brain (as previously thought), but in each cell of your body which communicates information and helps make decisions for your whole being. The same neuropeptides are found not only in the brain, but also in the heart, in the immune system and all through the body." Meaning emotions affect your whole being positively or negatively, depending on what you're thinking and therefore feeling.

These techniques interrupt the stress response and show you how to instantly shift your thoughts and feelings to a higher level that is congruent with your body-mind's integrity and well-being.

You are consciously tapping into the body's innate ability to heal itself mentally, emotionally, physically and energetically. As your emotions and biochemistry change, your perceptions about yourself, your work, your relationships, your life, your beliefs and priorities change."

Energy Medicine techniques for Instant Stress Release

Donna Eden is a leading authority and practitioner in the field of Energy Medicine. As she states in her great book *Energy Medicine*, "Energy medicine is safe, natural and accessible. It is both contemporary and ancient. Energy medicine is the best term I know for describing the understanding of the body as a system of energies that is applied for promoting health, healing and happiness."

Energy medicine uses the body's energy systems to automatically heal mentally, emotionally and physically. As Donna says, "Using the principals of energy medicine, you can optimize your body's natural capacities to heal itself. You can manage your energies to more effectively meet stress, reduce anxiety and free yourself of many ailments."

Donna has many effective exercises and techniques I have used over the years that have helped so many people, including myself. The following exercises of hers are some of my favorites because they offer instant stress release both at home and at work. These exercises are really great if you work at a computer for extended periods of time! They are more physical in application and a harmonious blend of body-mind-energy integration and healing.

You can find the following exercises, plus many more, in her book *Energy Medicine*.

A daily stress releasing energy routine

These techniques can be used to handle life's daily irritations and frustrations. Use them throughout the day to release stress, to feel energized, to think clearly and positively, to restore calmness, to quiet the mind and to feel strong and confident and not feel overwhelmed. They can even be done sitting at your desk.

The Thymus Tap

Tapping the thymus gland will do the following:

- **Clears and stimulates all of your energies (even under stress in negative situations)**
- **Strengthens your immune system (especially if you feel yourself catching a cold)**
- **Increases your clarity and vitality**

1. Place your fingertips on your sternum in the center of your chest.

2. Tap your thymus point for about 10 to 20 seconds. You will feel yourself becoming clear and centered.

The K-27 Tap

Tapping and/or massaging your K-27 points will do the following:

- **Energize you if you are feeling tired or sluggish**
- **Help you to think more clearly and be able to focus and concentrate**

1. Place your fingertips on your clavicle (collarbone) and slide them toward the center where it stops. Drop your fingers down an inch and slightly outward to a small indentation.

2. Tap and/or massage these points firmly for about 10 to 20 seconds.
   If you can't use both hands, use your thumb and fingers of one hand to do both points at the same time.

3. Continue massaging along under your clavicle (especially points that are sore until you reach your shoulder bone. Then massage down and under the armpit.

Instant Energy Lift

Restoring energy flow to the head will do the following:

- **Clear your thinking**
- **Energize you**
- **Clear and center your energies**

1. Place your finger on your chin. Slide it under your chin to an indent that is there. With either the other hand, or the little finger on the same hand, place that finger on the top of your sternum.

2. Hold this connection until you feel energy flowing up into your head. It will immediately energize you. It is very powerful.

Releasing Stress and Thinking Clearly

The next series of exercises are great for restoring energy and blood flow to the head to think more clearly and to release stress tension and anxiety.

Stress Relief: Releasing Facial Tension

This exercise will do the following:

- **Release facial tension and restore energy and blood flow**
- **Relieve sinus congestion and headaches**

1. Place your thumbs under and against your cheekbones. Push upward firmly.

2. Place your middle fingers on the bridge of your nose. Press in firmly and hold. These sinus points will usually be sore.

3. Next slide your middle fingers up slightly. Now slide them slowly across your forehead into your temples. Repeat this as many times as needed. This feels so good!

Stress Relief: Releasing Facial, Head, Neck and Shoulder Tension

This exercise will do the following:

- **Opens, flows and unblocks your energy**
- **Releases tension and restores blood flow**
- **Allows you to think clearly and energizes you**

1. Place your fingertips just under and against your cheekbones. Push in and upwards firmly. Slowly push your fingers up along your cheekbone up into your temples over the ears. Continue either pushing in with your fingers, or by massaging back down behind your ears and along the curve of the skull until your fingers meet at your neck (the atlas).

2. At this point you can proceed in one of two ways: Place your fingers on your neck on either side of the vertebrae. Massage downward on the knots that are usually there. Continue on down to the back as far as you can reach.
Or
Lay one hand over your opposite shoulder. Slide this hand up the back of your neck. Push in and pull your fingers forward towards the front of your neck. Continue on down and over your shoulder with the forward pulling motion. Do this three times on each side.

Ear Pull

This exercise does the following:

- **Energizes you and stimulates blood flow**
- **Makes you feel good**

1. With your thumb and forefinger gently tug and massage your ear. Start at the top of your ear where it joins your head. Work all the way down your ear ending at the lobe.

2. Repeat three times on each ear.

The Crown Pull

This exercise does the following:

- **Calms your mind and nervous system**
- **Restores energy flow and opens crown chakra**
- **Clears headaches**

1. Place your thumbs on your temples on each side of your head. Rest your fingertips on the center of your forehead.

2. Slowly and firmly pull your fingers toward your temples stretching the skin. Repeat the stretch.

3. Continue this pattern all across the top and down the back of your head.

4. Continue down the back of your neck and as far down your back as you can reach.

The Arm Stretch

This exercise does the following:

- **Opens the meridians and energy flow**
- **Releases toxic energies**
- **Reduces tension and makes you feel good**

1. Stand with your hands together in a prayer position at your chest.

2. Stretch your arm up as high over your head as you can reach. Flatten your hand back and push up. Stretch your other arm down. Flatten your hand back and push down.

3. Switch arms and repeat the stretch ending with your hands in a prayer position at your chest.

Cross Over Exercises for Clearing, Calming and Stress Relief

The left hemisphere of your brain needs to send information to the right side of your body and the right hemisphere needs to send information to the left side. If the energy of each hemisphere is not adequately crossing over to the opposite side, your body and brain cannot function properly. Also the body's ability to heal itself is greatly hampered. The following exercises allow you to reestablish the crossover pattern so your whole system can function effectively and your body can heal naturally again.

The Cross Crawl

This exercise does the following:

- **Feel balanced and think more clearly**
- **Improve your coordination**
- **Harmonize your energies**

1. While standing or even sitting, lift your right arm and left leg at the same time.

2. Next lift your left arm and your right leg at the same time. (If you have trouble doing this, try touching your raised arm to the opposite knee.)

3. Repeat, exaggerating the movements so your arms swing over to the opposite side of your body.

4. Continue in this exaggerated march for at least 30 seconds.

The Big Figure 8 Movement

This exercise does the following:

- **Energetically integrates the right and left hemispheres of the brain**
- **Helps align the energy systems to work in harmony throughout the body**
- **Helps with dyslexia, learning disabilities and immune dysfunction**
- **Clears thinking and is calming and centering**

1. Standing, begin swaying your body and your arms in a figure eight motion. Let your arms swing out wide and freely to each side. Continue for at least 30 seconds.

Eye Tracking

This exercise does the following:

- **Clears thinking and is calming and centering**
- **Releases the emotional charge from past memories**

1. Put your palms together with your thumbs up. Raise your arms to eye level.

2. Move your hands back and forth in a horizontal figure eight.

3. While holding your head still, look at your thumbs and let your eyes track them back and forth.

The Wayne Cook Posture

This exercise (named after a pioneer in bioenergetic force fields) does the following:

- **Calms and centers you when you feel stressed and overwhelmed mentally, emotionally and/or physically**
- **Helps you to learn more proficiently and assimilate information**
- **Quiets your mind so you can stop thinking unwanted thoughts**

1. Sitting down, place your right foot over your left knee. Put your left hand around your right ankle and your right hand around the ball of your right foot.

2. Relaxing, gently pull your right leg toward you creating a stretch. Remain here until you feel a centering taking place.

3. Switch legs. Place your left foot over your right knee. Put your right hand around your left ankle and you left hand around the ball of your left foot. Repeat the stretch with your left leg.

Reprogramming Your Beliefs and Habit Field Clearing

A *habit field is a field of energy that holds the habitual patterns of your beliefs, thoughts and behavior.* Whatever was originally imprinted into it is the way it wants it to stay. Although your habit field resists change vigorously, it is possible for it to be altered with certain energy techniques. When the habit field shifts, shifts in beliefs, thoughts, behavior and physiological conditions also occur. Because the triple warmer meridian (an important energy meridian) controls the body's habits, working with it can facilitate change in your habit field. The "temporal tap" is a method that is effectively used to break old habits and establish new ones, be they psychological or physiological habits. Tapping directly affects the neurological system and the habit energy field to be able to create the desired change.

Clearing your energies is necessary for the effective reprogramming of your habit field. When you are stressed, your vibratory level is low and your energies are scrambled and not crossing properly, it becomes very difficult to reprogram your beliefs and your habit field. Therefore applying any or all of the above exercises greatly facilitates in making the changes you desire.

Frontal Touch

Releasing the Negative Charge of a Traumatic Memory

This exercise does the following:

- **Removes the negative charge**
- **Breaks up the memory, the feeling and the defensive response in the habit field**

1. Select a memory from a past or current situation that is painful, overwhelming or negatively charged for you. Replay your bad memory.

2. As the memory starts playing, using both hands, place your thumbs on your temples and rest your fingers across the middle of your forehead. Hold these neu-rovascular points until the emotional charge from the memory has dissipated.

If you liked these exercises, read Donna Eden's incredible book, *Energy Medicine*.

In Summary

1. Achieving **Instant Stress Release** by using the fields of **Energy Psychology** and **Energy Medicine**. **Instant Stress Release** technology is based on how your body and mind are designed to heal when your thoughts, emotions, brain and biochemicals are affected by your energy systems and electromagnetic fields. It uses the best methods of both fields of Energy Psychology and Energy Medicine to help you live a life free of stress.

2. **Thought Field Therapy** is a branch of Energy Psychology that deals with the interrelationship between emotions, thoughts, behavior and the body's energy systems. By tapping specific points of the body's energy systems, emotional, mental and physical stress can be cleared. Limiting and negative beliefs, thoughts and habit patterns can be cleared or reprogrammed into ones that are congruent with your innate intelligence or Truth.

   Tapping and Eye Roll Technique is a highly effective method that releases the charged energy you experience in a negative situation. It also stimulates the brain to begin replacing the undesired habit pattern of negative thinking and feeling into a positive one instead.

   Frontal Cortex Automatic Calming and Centering is another very effective Energy Medicine technique. When you are majorly stressing, it initiates the brain and your body-mind to naturally heal itself by shifting your thoughts and emotions to those of health and well-being. Also by releasing repressed toxic emotionally charged energy so the body-mind can return to normal functioning.

3. **A Quick and Easy Daily Stress Releasing Energy Routine**
   These techniques by Donna Eden interrupt the stress
   response and show you how to instantly shift your thoughts
   and feelings to a higher level that is congruent with your
   body-mind's integrity and well-being.
   You are consciously tapping into the body's innate ability to
   heal itself mentally, emotionally, physically and energetically.
   "As your emotions and biochemistry change, your perceptions about yourself, your work, your relationships, your life,
   your beliefs and priorities change," states Donna Eden.

CHAPTER 5

How do I know which technique to use when?

Important concepts used in clearing the need to stress

S tress is caused by your lower-self ego not being able to control what it wants to control (which is everything). So it settles for controlling you instead. It controls how badly it can make you feel mentally, emotionally, physically, biochemically and energetically. The worse it makes you feel, the more power and control it thinks it has. If you choose to reintegrate your ego back home into your Soul, your reward is happiness, health, peace, clarity of thinking and the wisdom and love of your Soul. Then you can live your life being happy and healthy and wealthy and free.

You are designed with many ways to override or transcend ego. Use the following methods to experience how they work, then use the ones that work best for you.

Here are three ways to transcend your ego:
1. Know that you are **naturally designed to override your ego.** The techniques that specifically help do this are the Frontal

Touch, the Prove it to me…and the NOW WHAT…Or you can use any of the Exit Loops Out of ego methods.

2. **Since ego can *only* control you when your energy is contracted and your vibratory level is low,** it behooves you to **keep your vibratory level high by expanding your energy and aligning with High Energies** beginning with your own Soul. There are many exercises to do this such as:

   • Aligning with High Functioning Energy and Divine Source Energy

   • Sigh…Look Up…Expand four feet up and forty feet out

   • Any of the Exit Loops Out of ego exercises will also do raise your vibration high enough so you won't access ego

3. **Ego tells lies that make you fear and worry,** such as the "What if…" fears. Then it releases bad-feeling biochemicals to make sure you believe that its lies are true thus deepening the fear and worry. Your logic and True-Self are telling you the lies are false, but your emotions feel they are true. Nine out of ten times emotions win. But **you can counteract the bad feeling biochemicals simply by commanding your ego or Knowing to release into your body and mind the good feeling emotional up-lifters such as *endorphins, serotonin and L-dopamine.***

When to use the tools you've learned

There are four basic categories where you can use the tools and exercises you've learned. There are certain times, conditions or situations when specific exercises and methods or certain combinations are more expedient than others. Here are the basic categories:

1. **Shifting out of negative ego and into Soul to be clear and confident.**

Example: For this you could use the "Sigh… Look Up…Expand your energy up 4 feet and out 40 feet" exercise.

2. **Aligning with High Energies and/or Specific Energies internally and externally to help you.**
Example: Call to you Resolution Energy to help resolve your problems. Or call to you the Specific Energies to help you with anything you want, like changing the need to stress habit pattern.

3. **Giving commands (to your ego or yourself) so you regain control of your lower self.**
Example: *"Ego release endorphins, serotonin and L-dopamine NOW!"*
This instantly counteracts the biochemicals it previously released to make you feel bad so you'd believe its lies to make you feel even worse.
Example: Using "I choose…"phrases are very powerful such as: **"I choose happiness, clarity, peace, divine wisdom and strength instead!"**

4. **Instant Stress Release techniques for the body and mind that tend to be more physically applied.**
Example: **Opening and clearing your chakras** so you can function without heavy mental and physical stress.
Example: Do the **Thymus tap…**on your sternum in the center of your chest, followed by the **K27 massage…**on the sore points right under your collar bone to get your systems running again and be clear and grounded. Any of Donna Eden's exercises are great for this.

All of the above methods and techniques are great to do at work (especially if you work with computers) or at home, or in social settings or in challenging situations and relationships. Anytime you want to feel good, but don't, use these techniques. *Use these techniques every time you begin to feel stressed to interrupt and break the "I need to feel stressed" habit pattern.* If you need to use them 100 times a day, *use them!* The more consistently you use them, (like every day) the happier and healthier you'll be to create the life you really want.

Fail Safe Tools

If you're not sure which technique to use, you can use these specific "go to" techniques because they work for every situation. There are many exercises that fit the same situation…it's your choice which tools you want to use. Try them and play with them to see what works best for you.

Here are my favorite techniques for just about any situation to shift out of ego and into Soul so you can think clearly and act wisely.

The following methods are my favorite "fail safe tools" for everything including Instant Stress Release and Resolution Solving.

Combination of Instant Stress Release Techniques

1. **Sigh…look up** until the emotional charge goes away…and **expand 4 feet up and 40 feet out**

2. **Thymus Tap**…followed by the **K27 massage**…to get your systems running again and be clear and grounded

3. Say, **"DO I WANT TO FEEL THIS THIS BADLY?…NO"**…

   Then say, **"I CHOOSE happiness, clarity, ease of being, divine wisdom and strength INSTEAD!"**
   Notice how powerful and clear you feel now…

4. Align with High Energies to help you…With palms

The Next Step Up

up, Say, **"Divine Source Energy be here now"**...
Feel the peace, clarity and power of this beautiful
energy..." Then say, **"High Functioning Energy be
here now..."** Feel clarity and strength of this strong
energy...

5. Call to you **Resolution Energy**. Put your problem into
    the energy and say, **"**(State the problem) **Problem I
    put you into Resolution Energy to work out in the
    highest, easiest and most loving and appropriate
    way for all concerned...especially me!"** Feel how all
    the stress is gone and the burden has lifted...

6. **Then *imagine* how it feels when the problem is
    all resolved...This last step is important because
    it's this energy that creates the resolution!...**
    Experience how clear and happy you feel...**Remember
    how many times this has worked for you in the
    past.**

7. **Clear** the **negative feelings** and **transition ego back
    into the heart of your Soul:**

    Imagine placing your ego into your palms then placing
    one on top of the other...Move your hands slowly toward
    your heart...As your palms touch your heart, breathe your
    ego into the heart of your soul...to become one with soul.
    Feel how clear and peaceful you are now...

For persistent ego fears use "Prove it to me" (Exit Loop 4)
and "NOW WHAT" (Exit Loop 7):

Exit Loop 4

Clearing the "what ifs…" with "Prove to me your lie is true!"

Ego will tell you any lie to get you to feel weak and powerless so it can control you. It's favorite fear and worry tactic is to say to you, **"what if** something's wrong…**what if** you aren't good enough…**what if** they don't like you…**what if** it won't work…what if……. As soon as ego starts with the **"what ifs…"** You say to it, **"Prove to me your lie is true!"** It never can, because it always lies. You can feel ego receding immediately. If you **consistently interrupt** it with **"Prove it to me"**, it won't want to use the "what if…" tactic any more.

Exit Loop 6

Confronting and Clearing Ego with "NOW WHAT"

When ego is making you fear say, **"OK, ego suppose you're right…NOW WHAT?"** Ego will immediately back off and recede because it was lying and you just took its power away. **Any time you use sarcasm, you assume the powerful dominate position.**

Check to see if there's any remaining fear. If there is, check to see what the percentages are…Example: 80% gone, 20% still there. Continue repeating the exercise until the fear is completely gone.

An instant way to release stress is doing the Soul Fountain (Exit Loop 5)

Soul Fountain

Clearing Negative Thoughts, Feelings & Energies

This exercise is especially good if you're in a toxic situation, or around a person firmly rooted in ego, or after an argument with someone.

Give a big sigh, look up, and expand 4 feet up and 40 feet out.

Imagine your Soul's light and love flowing up and out of you like a fountain. As the light flows up and out of every pore, it takes with it negative energies and toxins that have been suppressed...leaving you feeling clear and refreshed...with a deep feeling of well-being. Do this as many times as needed throughout the day. Remember to do this at night right before you fall asleep. You'll have a good night's sleep.

Opening and Clearing Your Chakras

To open your chakras, manually place your fingertips over your **Heart Chakra**, and then extend your arms all the way out with palms turned up. Open and close them rapidly until your chakras begin to open and clear. Next do the same with your **Throat Chakra**, then your **Third Eye Chakra**, then your **Crown Chakra** (located on the top of your head), then your **Solar Plexus Chakra** (about 3 inches above your naval), then your **Sacral Chakra** and finally your **Root Chakra** (about 3 inches below your naval).

Chakras are major energy vortex centers. They're like spinning wheels of energy located in the midline of your body.

There are seven major chakras and many more minor ones. When your chakras are not open and flowing with energy, you cannot function well mentally, emotionally, physically or energetically. It especially compromises your immune system.

Your **Crown Chakra** helps you to be fully connected spiritually, especially with energies of light and love. It's located on the top of your head.

Your **Third Eye** Chakra deals in inspiration, imagination, wisdom and comprehension in totalities. It's located in the center of your forehead.

Your **Throat Chakra** helps you to communicate and express yourself. It is located in the throat area.

Your **Heart Chakra** helps you experience the highest forms of love. It is located in your chest just above your heart.

Your **Solar Plexus Chakra** deals with emotions, self-confidence and self-worth issues. It is located in the stomach area of your abdomen.

Your **Sacral Chakra** deals with pleasure, sexuality, connection to others and new experiences. It is located about 2 to 3 inches below the naval.

Your **Root Chakra** helps you feel grounded and stable. It is located at the base of your spine or tailbone.

Frontal Touch

Another favorite stress release technique is putting your fingers across your forehead and thumbs on temples. Think about your problem until suddenly the negative charge about it just dissolves.

For instant clarity I use the following affirmations for myself all the time. They're very powerful and resonate with Truth Energy.

I choose happiness, clarity, peace, light and love
and divine wisdom instead!
I choose being happy and healthy and wealthy and free.
That's me!

These next exercises by Donna Eden work really well to give you energy and release stress. (These techniques are especially great if you work at a computer.)

Ear Pull

This exercise does the following:

- **Energizes you and stimulates blood flow**
- **Makes you feel good**

1. With your thumb and forefinger gently tug and massage your ear. Start at the top of your ear where it joins your head. Work all the down your ear ending at the lobe.

2. Repeat 3 times on each ear.

The Crown Pull

This exercise does the following:

- **Calms your mind and nervous system**
- **Restores energy flow and opens crown chakra**
- **Clears headaches**

1. Place your thumbs on your temples on each side of your head. Rest your fingertips on the center of your forehead.

2. Slowly and firmly pull your fingers toward your temples stretching the skin. Repeat the stretch.

3. Continue this pattern all across the top and down the back of your head.

4. Continue down the back of your neck and as far down

The next series of exercises are excellent to calm, center and clear your mind so you can think clearly.

The Cross Crawl

This exercise does the following:

- **Feel balanced and think more clearly**
- **Improve your coordination**
- **Harmonize your energies**

1. While standing or even sitting, lift your right arm and left leg at the same time.

2. Next lift your left arm and your right leg at the same time. (If you have trouble doing this try touching your raised arm to the opposite knee.)

3. Repeat, exaggerating the movements so your arms swing over to the opposite side of your body.

4. Continue in this exaggerated march for at least 30 seconds.

The Big Figure 8 Movement

This exercise does the following:

- **Energetically integrates the right and left hemispheres of the brain**
- **Helps align the energy systems to work in harmony throughout the body**
- **Treats dyslexia, learning disabilities and immune dysfunction**
- **Clears thinking and is calming and centering**

Standing, begin swaying your body and your arms in a figure eight motion. Let your arms swing out wide and freely to each side. Continue for at least 30 seconds.

Eye Tracking

This exercise does the following:

- **Clears thinking and is calming and centering**
- **Releases the emotional charge from past memories**

1. Put your palms together with your thumbs up. Raise your arms to eye level.

2. Move your hands back and forth in a horizontal figure eight.

3. While holding your head still, look at your thumbs and let your eyes track them back and forth.

The Wayne Cook Posture

This exercise (named after a pioneer in bioenergetic force fields) does the following:

- **Calms and centers you when you feel stressed and overwhelmed mentally, emotionally and/or physically**

- **Helps you to learn more proficiently and assimilate information**
- **Quiets your mind so you can stop thinking unwanted thoughts**

1. Sitting down, place your right foot over your left knee. Put your left hand around your right ankle and your right hand around the ball of your right foot.

2. Relaxing, gently pull your right leg toward you creating a stretch. Remain here and feel a centering taking place.

3. Switch legs. Place your left foot over your right knee. Put your right hand around your left ankle and you left hand around the ball of your left foot. Repeat the stretch with your left leg.

4. Uncross your legs and place your fingertips together forming a pyramid. Place your thumbs to rest on the center of your forehead. Slowly separate your thumbs across your forehead, pulling the skin.

5. Bring your thumbs back to the center of your forehead. With your hands in a prayer position, slowly lower them in front of you. Experience how calm and centered you now feel.

In closing...

It was fun writing this book. I hope it helps you in your every day life. Remember **you** get to choose what you want to think and feel, not your ego. You now have the tools to override your ego's habit patterns of making you feel stressed. Now you can shift out of worry and into clarity and calm every time you choose. Even when your ego makes you think you don't want to do these techniques and exercises, override your ego and DO THEM ANYWAY because they really work. The more you use them, the better your life will be in every way.

Remember how good it feels to align with energy to help you create what you want or to clear what you don't want! It's pretty amazing how happy and powerful you feel when calling to you and aligning with High Functioning Energy or Divine Source Energy. Especially aligning with the Light and Love of your own Soul's energy is awesome. But most of all remember...

Be clear about what you want...
Align with the energies for it...
Expect Miracles...

The End...
of this book
And the beginning of your
new stress free life!

Have fun creating the life you really want!

For information about phone sessions or a series of phone sessions with Barbara or any of The Next Step Up Programs, Workshops and Training Seminars which include:

- Improving Relationships
- The Art of Instant Stress Release
- Making Transitions Easy
- Happiness, Health and Healing
- Business Stress Management

You can contact me at Energy Therapeutic Solutions at etsforyou.com.

Warmly,
Barbara